EQUIPPED FOR ADVENTURE

SCOTT KIRBY

new
hope
PUBLISHERS

Birmingham, Alabama

New Hope® Publishers
P. O. Box 12065
Birmingham, AL 35202-2065
www.newhopepublishers.com

ISBN-10: 1-59669-011-9
ISBN-13: 978-1-59669-011-0

N064143•0806•3M1

CONTENTS

"Life is either a daring adventure . . . or nothing."—Helen Keller

INTRODUCTION

THE ADVENTURE BEGINS

"Before, I had a *head* for missions. Now I have a *heart* for missions." My friend almost wept as he shared this testimony with our church. What happened? He had just arrived home from his first global short-term mission trip and the experience had changed his life. His experience is not uncommon.

> "We're forever changed."
> "This has been the number one experience of my life."
> "Nothing has ever moved me like this visit."
> "I did not realize how I would be touched."
> "It's the best thing I have ever done in my whole life."

You are probably reading this book because you are already interested in global missions. You also probably believe that the Great Commission (Matthew 28:18–20) and Acts 1:8 call us to do more than just give our money and pray. You believe that our churches should be personally involved in global missions. It should be the heartbeat of the local church.

But you struggle with a giant problem. Most of the people in your church really are not interested. They are interested in local needs and issues. Only about 2 percent of the average church's income goes to international missions and most churches have never sent out a missionary. Our churches have a head for missions, but not a heart.

So what can we do? How do we help people to develop a heart for the world? How do we interest and personally involve people in global missions? Preaching and teaching on missions is not enough. The best way to infect people with a heart for the world is through firsthand exposure to missions and missionaries through short-term mission experiences. Missions becomes real to people when they go. Mission vision is more caught than taught.

To reawaken our churches to their global responsibilities, church leadership and lay ministers must prioritize sending short-term mission teams from our local churches. But how do we do it?

Let's Get Started

This book is designed to help you become involved in the short-term mission adventure. Church leaders, individuals, and team leaders/organizers will find this material useful. Church leaders will find research and information to keep a missions mind-set before their congregations. The solo short-termer will find practical help as he prepares for his trip. The team leader/organizer will discover how to organize, train, and effectively lead a short-term mission team.

The book is organized in two sections:
1. Why do short-term missions? (chaps. 1–4) and
2. How to organize, train, and lead teams (chaps. 5–14).

The first section covers the philosophy behind missions. It reviews the trends of American culture and how culture impacts people's outlook on missions. It also reminds church leaders about the importance of being involved with God globally. The second section offers practical advice and steps for planning, participating, and follow up for short-term mission trips. If you already understand the importance of short-term missions, skip the first section and begin with the second section.

THE ADVENTURE OF A LIFETIME!

The short-term mission adventure? Why use the word *adventure* with short-term missions?

Indiana Jones? Eating bugs in Africa? Savage cannibals cooking missionaries for dinner? Sorry to disappoint you, but there is a different kind of adventure in mind. Webster's dictionary defines *adventure* as "an unusual, stirring, or challenging experience." Going on a short-term trip, or organizing and leading a team of mission rookies halfway around the world to serve God in obedience to the Great Commission is the kind of adventure described in the following pages. You'll go to new places, experience new cultures, meet new friends, and have new experiences. You and the people on your team will be challenged and changed. You'll find yourself on the front lines of what God is doing and you'll see Him use you and your team. What could be more adventuresome than that? So, fasten your seat belt, stow your tray table, put your seat in the upright position, and prepare to take off on the short-term mission adventure!

CHAPTER 1

SHORT-TERM: A NEW ERA IN MISSIONS

God is doing something new. Short-term missions is the most exciting development in recent missions history. It has come about due to many reasons, but one very important reason is the culture and generational changes in our American churches. It is no longer the 1950s and things are very, very different.

Our churches today have several different generational groups: builders, boomers, busters, and bridgers. A generation is a group of people who are connected by their place in time with common boundaries, values, and experiences. These groupings are generally delineated in terms of age, but the real difference is in terms of attitude. They think differently! The implications of these generational differences to missions mobilization are enormous.

> ## Generational Slogans
> **Builders:** "Be sure."
> **Boomers:** "Just do it."
> **Busters:** "Whatever!"
> **Bridgers:** "If it feels good, it's all right, so do it."

Builders are the generation born before 1945. Their formative influences were the Great Depression, rural lifestyle, World War II, Pearl Harbor, no television, and big band music. They are loyal, hardworking, patriotic, frugal, and cautious. They are characterized by stability, sacrifice, self-denial, conformity, and conservatism. Builders are declining in terms of numbers and influence due to aging and failing health that leads to death.

Boomers are those born between 1946 and 1964. Their name comes from the huge surge of births following World War II called the baby boom. They are the largest group and now make up over half of all American wage earners. Their formative influences include television, the cold war, rock and roll, the murders of John Kennedy and Martin Luther King Jr., the space race, Vietnam, Watergate, the civil rights movement, and shopping malls. They are often independent and entrepreneurial. They often value personal success, economic well-being, family life, and education. Many distrust institutions, are more nonconformist, and are tolerant of diversity.

Busters are those born between 1965 and 1983 (also called Generation X). During this period, the baby boom slowed or went bust, thus the name busters. They can be stereotyped by the TV show, *Friends*. Their formative influences include divorce, blended families, *Roe v. Wade*, computers, video games, terrorism, and AIDS. They tend to be somewhat cynical, disconnected, and insecure. They often fear the future, reject absolute truth, and feel alone and unsure. Many suffer pain because almost 50 percent come from divorced homes. They place great value on peer relationships.

Bridgers are those born after 1983. They are also called postmoderns, millennial generation, or mosaics. They were born into a burgeoning technological age and computers, personal cell phones, and credit cards are taken for granted. Commitment and responsibility are rare. Relationships, friendships, entertainment, and things that make them feel good are important.

EQUIPPED FOR ADVENTURE

THE CHANGING CHURCH

These four different groups help us understand why the American church is changing and how that change is affecting the world missions task.

Traditionally, the older builder generation has strongly supported international missions. They both funded and staffed global missions efforts because they believed in the importance of the global missions effort. But we are now faced with a big problem. The older generation is aging and younger baby boomers and even busters are replacing their leadership roles in the churches. These boomers don't hold the same values as the older builder generation—especially in relation to missions. A landmark study of evangelical Christian baby boomers by James Engel and Jerry D. Jones published in 1989 shook up the evangelical mission leadership community. They found that only 10 percent of Christian boomers showed any significant interest in overseas missions. Fifty percent were not interested at all! Evangelical missions leaders finally woke up to the fact that they had a big problem. They had wrongly assumed that boomers would feel the same about missions as the older generation.

Not long ago, 1,400 Southern Baptist pastors, church staff, and key lay leaders were asked to rank seven key ministry areas in order of the priority in which they wanted their churches to be involved at the beginning of the twenty-first century. Home and international missions came in dead last!

Let's face the facts. The American church is rapidly accepting an isolationist worldview. Missions is no longer a priority in the local church—no matter how much lip service we may give to it. We are now more focused on personal concerns. Causes which are closer to home are overwhelmingly given the support that at one time would have gone to international missions. Ask any missionary recruit trying to raise financial support and you will hear how hard it is. It is much harder than it was 40 years ago. Mission statistician David Barrett documents that Christians are spending less than one dollar per every thousand earned for global missions efforts. The American missions movement is stagnating. New missionary recruitment is declining. Existing funding resources are eroding—especially from local churches. Much of this decline is a reflection of boomer apathy towards global missions causes.

The North American church is having a diminishing role in global evangelism while the missionary forces from other countries are growing dramatically. The "from the West to the Rest" mode has changed. The axis of world missionary expansion has shifted from the West to the East and from the North to the South. We are doing less at a time when we should be doing more. This is no time for business as usual. We must find some way to reawaken the missionary heart of the church.

> "Let us be honest and admit that at present, only a tiny percentage of believers are really taking ownership of the Great Commission."—George Verwer

In order to reach the world with the gospel, we must understand our changing culture and adapt our ways of doing things. We must either change or die! Churches should not change our message. We can never change our message. However, we must be constantly changing our method. A changing church in a changing culture demands a constantly changing strategy. Trying to promote global missions among boomers, busters, and bridgers the same way we have always done it with the older builder generation is like trying to put new wine in old wineskins. It simply won't work. Church leaders must understand the age wave and that we are no longer living in the 1950s. Ozzie and Harriet don't live here anymore! The Scriptures say that the men of Issachar were men "who understood the times and knew what Israel should do" (1 Chronicles 12:32). We are living in a new era and we must be wise people who also understand our times and what to do. We must learn new ways for new days.

FOUR CONTEMPORARY CHURCH MODELS

Most American churches fall into one of four patterns in relation to global missions: isolationist, supporting, sending, or partnering.

ISOLATIONIST. These churches have very little to do with global missions. They may range from the suburban boomer church that is utterly focused on its own local outreach to the rural church that has simply never supported anything beyond its own four walls. Or, they may be churches whose theology leads them not to be supportive of global missions. The problem with the isolationist model is simple. It is just unbiblical! It blatantly ignores the commands of Christ to bring the gospel to all peoples.

SUPPORTING. The supporting church has an interest in global missions, but the role of the local church is primarily understood as giving passive financial and prayer support. These churches are usually dependent upon missions agencies to do global missions. They have delegated to the denominational missions agency the responsibility of global missions and their own missions involvement is usually impersonal. They send their money to the denominational missions organization and that's it. Perhaps 90 percent of American evangelical churches fall into this category. They continue to practice this pattern as they have done the last 50 years with their eyes shut to the changing culture around them.

Mission support in these churches is headed for a serious crisis, however. Here is the problem: International missions have been supported primarily by the older generation. Baby boomers, however, are far less interested in missions as it is practiced under

> **www.postmission.com:** A resource for missions agency leaders who are anxious to bridge the gap with their younger colleagues and "for anyone who wants to find out about the implications of Postmodernity for Christian Mission."

the supporting model. The institutional approach and lack of personalization turns them off. Baby boomers are now assuming church leadership as the older generation dies off or moves aside, and missions interest and financial support is therefore now declining. The churches are turning more to things nearer at home—which is a reflection of boomer values. Unless something happens to reverse the trend, these churches will dramatically decrease their involvement in global missions in the coming years. The change will happen more quickly among city and suburban churches than in rural and small-town churches.

There is another problem with the supporting model—a doctrinal problem. God has given the task of global evangelism to the local church (Acts 13:1–3). The supporting model is not acceptable because it relinquishes to a missions organization the responsibility of the local church to be personally involved in global evangelization.

SENDING. These churches are energetically involved in global missions and the local church itself becomes the missions agency or creates its own agency(s). They have a vision to recruit, train, and send out their own people. They recognize that God has given the local church the responsibility of global evangelism and believe that the local church cannot delegate this responsibility. They want ownership of missions and believe that the local church is the primary sending agency.

Churches in this model are often motivated by dissatisfaction or suspicion of existing missions organizations. They reflect a lessening commitment to denominationalism and a mistrust of institutionalism. Most of these are churches not closely affiliated with a denomination. Aggressive and entrepreneurial boomers who want to find more productive and strategic channels for their mission support lead these churches. They often perceive existing missions agencies as only interested in the local church's money, backward in strategy, and unresponsive to reaching the neediest areas of the world.

Sending churches are missions-active and are doing some great things. However, their weakness is that their very independence inhibits cooperation in missions which ultimately hinders the task of global evangelism. Their lack of cooperation prevents them from being used most effectively as part of a cooperative plan and strategy. Also, their usefulness is hindered because they constantly have to reinvent the wheel. They fail to benefit from the experience, expertise, and accountability of existing missions organizations. These churches fail to grasp that so much more can be done cooperatively than independently.

PARTNERING. This last style incorporates the strengths of the sending model without the weakness of independence. Like the sending model, partnering churches believe in the responsibility of the local church to be actively and personally involved in global missions—far beyond just giving money. They therefore look for ways to involve their members personally in global missions.

But they also recognize that more can be done cooperatively in partnership than in isolation. They believe that we all need to work together to reach the world. They see global missions in terms of partnership. How can our church partner with our denominational missions organization, other missions agencies, other churches, missionaries, nationals, and national churches in order to get the job done? Partnering churches don't give up their personal involvement, but they do look for ways to do it cooperatively—in order to maximize efforts.

These churches also recognize the changes happening in the non-Western church and want to be active partners. They recognize the changing US missionary role. This often means supporting non-Western national ministries in addition to supporting Western missionaries and organizations. They recognize that the immense task of global evangelization is not going to be accomplished by only Anglo American missionaries. We must partner with churches and national ministries in other countries in order to get the job done.

The *American Heritage Dictionary* defines *partnership* as "a relationship between individuals or groups that is characterized by mutual cooperation and responsibility, as for the achievement of a specified goal." Partnership in the best sense involves contributing vision, empowerment, facilitation, cooperation, resources, and specialized skills. Wise partnerships do not foster ongoing dependency. True partners are servants, not masters. Partnership is so important in missions that chapter 4 is completely devoted to this subject.

NEW ROLE FOR DENOMINATIONAL AND PARACHURCH MISSIONS AGENCIES

These changes in the American church mean that there must be a major repositioning and reevaluation of the whole role and work of mission boards. The need for missions agencies has not changed. But the way that they relate to the local church must change. Agencies who expect to work with this new generation of churches must begin to see themselves as partners with and servants to the local church. Agencies must recognize the restored primacy and priority of the local church—not just in theory, but also in practice. The Great Commission was not given to missions agencies, but to the local church. The role of missions agencies is to serve the local church by helping it to fulfill its missions mandate. Missions agency representatives must let the churches tell the agencies how they can help instead of the agencies telling the churches what to do. Missions agencies must work on being perceived as promoting a kingdom agenda instead of just a narrow denominational or agency agenda. They must also be perceived as cooperating with other groups who are also trying to fulfill the Great Commission. Agencies must become servants to the church. They must communicate the attitude, "Let's be partners. How can we help you? How can we enhance and facilitate your church's involvement and help fulfill your vision." Missions agencies can no longer just expect the local church's support. Now they must earn it.

Missions agencies must also demonstrate flexibility in relating to the local church. They cannot expect or force churches to fit into their missions mold. They must work together with each individual local church to create a personalized, strategic local church missions plan. They must work to provide ways that local churches can become personally involved in missions and sense ownership.

In the past, the focus of the agencies has been on the overseas mission and missionaries of the agency. This is as it should be. But, the result has been that missions agencies have often neglected or not related well to the supporting churches. Agencies must refocus attention on relating well to the local churches as partners. This may mean some significant reallocation of resources. It may cost time and energy that will seem at first glance to be better used overseas. If it is not done, however, then there will be no overseas work to support because there will be no new missionaries and no new money for the missions work.

REAWAKENING THE MISSIONS HEART OF THE CHURCH

The breakdown in global missions in North America is happening at the local church level. It is happening because we have not understood and responded to how the changing culture has altered the church. Missions today is primarily being supported by the older generation. As this generation passes from the scene, we are going to be in big trouble unless some way is found to reawaken the missionary heart of the younger people. Local churches and missions agencies cannot continue to practice, support, and promote missions the way they did it 40 years ago. The 1950s missions model may work for the seniors in your church, but it is not going to work for your boomers, busters, and bridgers. Local church leaders must wrestle with new ways and models to interest the younger generations in missions or their missions programs will slowly die. We cannot continue to live in the past. We must use new ways to reach a new generation with the challenge of the task of global evangelization. We must find a new way to reawaken the missionary heart of the church in this generation.

> "This generation wants to experience things before they're willing to commit to things."—Tamara Baker

Short-Term: A New Era in Missions

The changing American church has given rise to a new movement that is revolutionizing the way Americans think about missions and has launched a new era in missions. This new era is characterized by the belief that the Great Commission is not given only to missionary organizations. It is given to the entire church! As a result, the entire church should and can be personally involved in global evangelization. This new era is characterized by short-term volunteer involvement overseas in global mission efforts by local church members. It is nothing less than a grassroots missions revolution occurring in the American church. This new involvement of lay volunteers in missions is helping to reawaken the slumbering missionary heart of the church. God is doing something new!

What is short-term missions? Short-term missions involves non-vocational missionary volunteers who do specific tasks for predetermined, limited periods of time, usually in a cross-cultural setting, with definite spiritual objectives. Please note carefully the five elements of this definition.

> "Young people, including Christians, are hungry for risk and adventure, are comfortable in the global village, and have a global vision and awareness unrivalled by previous generations."—Richard Tiplady

- ✓ Nonvocational missionary volunteers
- ✓ Specific tasks
- ✓ Predetermined, limited periods of time
- ✓ Cross-cultural setting
- ✓ Definite spiritual objectives

The growing short-term missions movement appeals to the values that are important to the changing American church—values such as personal involvement, personal experience, relationship, and ownership. Short-term missions provides a channel for personalized involvement in global evangelization. It provides exciting, specific, goal-oriented, and time-limited opportunities for ministry with accomplishable objectives.

A Growing Movement

Nobody purposefully set out to create short-term missions as a strategic tool. Instead, this new era in missions has evolved over the years as a pragmatic response to a need and to an interest. Perhaps the major reason for the recent rise of the short-term missions movement has been the late twentieth-century advances that have made travel (especially air) easier, quicker, and cheaper. Short-term missions wasn't an option in William Carey's day. The boat trip to India alone took five months!

Of course there are many other factors that have also led to the growth of the short-term movement. These include the increase in personal discretionary time, increased personal wealth, and longer life spans. Also, improved communications between the international fields of service and churches here in the United States have contributed to the rapid rise of the short-term missions movement.

Short-term missions is now the fastest growing aspect of the American missionary movement. There is hardly an evangelical church in America that has not sent some of its people on short-term mission trips. Both young and old people, white-collar professionals and blue-collar workers are participating. Most denominational and independent missions organizations now have some sort of short-term program. Nobody really knows how many people go on short-term mission projects each year. It is estimated that Southern Baptists are now sending about 35,000 per year in association with their International Mission Board and probably this doesn't even include an equal number of Southern Baptist people who go on short-term teams independent of their International Mission Board. It is realistic to estimate that 1 million American believers participate in international short-term projects each year—and this tidal wave is growing rapidly. About two-thirds of these short-termers are going to Latin America. This is probably due to its proximity and the lower cost to travel there.

Is It Biblical?

There is no question that the modern short-term mission movement developed as a pragmatic response to a need and an interest. But is it just a fad, or is it biblical?

The phrase *short-term missions* is not found in the Bible. But neither are the words *missions, missionary, church planter, unreached people,* and many other words we use today. Although the word is not there, the concept of short-term missions is found many places in the Bible. Paul, for example, made short ministry visits to plant churches, encourage the local believers, and to bring financial assistance. God sent Philip the evangelist on a short-term mission trip to witness to the Ethiopian eunuch (Acts 8). Jesus sent the Twelve (Luke 9) and the Seventy-two (Luke 10) on short-term mission projects. God also sent Jonah on a short-term, evangelistic cross-cultural international mission trip to Nineveh—although the trip certainly was not voluntary!

Short-term missions finds its biblical support in the doctrine of the priesthood of the believer. This doctrine means that all believers are called to be witnesses (Acts 1:8; Matthew 28:18–20) and are equipped with spiritual gifts from the Holy Spirit for the work of building up the body of Christ (1 Corinthians 12). The Great Commission is not given to missions agencies. It is given to the church. It is given to all the church. In *Whatever It Takes*, Dub Jackson writes, "Matthew 28:19–20 was a directive for every Christian, not for a select few." All believers are to be involved in ministry (Ephesians 4:12) and in bringing the gospel to those who have not heard. There is no distinction made in the New Testament between clergy and laity. Also, there is no distinction made between the responsibility to be involved in ministry both locally and globally. We are to be involved both across the street and around the world (Acts 1:8; 8:1–4).

The New Testament reveals several missions models—all of which are valid and should be mutually complementary. For instance, one model involves the local church sending vocational missionaries on international missions assignments (Acts 11:22–24; 13:1–3). This corresponds to the contemporary role of the vocational missionary. This has been a primary international missions model throughout much of

"Yet quite subtly and unintentionally the missionary mandate that was committed by our Lord Jesus Christ Himself to the universal church . . . has been slowly, but surely, taken away. It has been taken away by the organizational church and the many and varied . . . mission boards, institutes and agencies. . . . To the degree, however that they have intentionally, or unintentionally, monopolized the missionary mandate by declaring the average member of the body of Christ ineligible, unqualified, and unworthy of the term missionary, they are to be faulted, for such is not the Biblical concept of missions."—Donald Kitchen church history due to the pragmatic realities of global travel and witness.

Although the vocational missionary certainly still holds a critical role, you may be surprised to discover that the New Testament offers yet another missions model. The New Testament offers no guidelines on the length of the missions project or the vocational status of the participant. Although no time limit is given, when Jesus sent His disciples out on mission trips, the impression is that the trips were of a relatively short duration (Luke 9:1ff.; and 10:1ff.). Furthermore, individual believers witnessed for Christ cross-culturally in the natural course of their movements from place to place (Acts 8:4; 11:19–21).

The contemporary short-term missions movement is both a biblical and a healthy expression of the American church's awakening awareness of its missionary responsibility. Global evangelization no longer needs to be only the work of the career missionary. Today, all believers may make a contribution. Biblically and practically, missions is becoming a teaming effort between the vocational missionary, the national believers, the American local church, and the short-term missionary.

"Our work always moved forward with the conviction that the only possible hope of sharing the gospel with the world was for the total church to become involved."—Dub Jackson

It is impossible not to see the hand of God in providing short-term missions as a tool for mobilizing this new generation for global evangelization. God knew that boomers, busters, and bridgers would be different. He knew their interests and what would capture their hearts and allegiance. And so it was at such a time as this that God allowed the short-term missions movement to blossom.

Dub Jackson is the acknowledged founder of short-term volunteer missions. He is a legend among those who do and study short-term missions. He says, "We came to recognize that every

Christian had to become involved and had to become involved now if we were to win a world. Career missionaries alone could never accomplish God's plan. . . . Looking back, it is hard to understand how we could have overlooked such an obvious and simple plan to share our love for our Lord with all whom He came to save!"

Short-term missions is not the answer to all the problems in missions today. It is, however, a valuable tool that God has given us at this time to help awaken and mobilize the American church to make the gospel of Christ known to the peoples of the world.

"A sight to take your breath away! Grand processions of people telling all the good things of God" (Romans 10:15 *The Message*).

CHAPTER 2

WHY YOUR CHURCH SHOULD GO

Why should you go on a short-term mission trip? Is it worth the time and money invested? What does it really accomplish? Is it something we ought to encourage? How can we evaluate the real value of short-term missions? It will cost significant money and consume a lot of energy and time. Is it worth it?

When we talk about assessing the value of short-term missions, we must first ask, "Value to whom?" Are we talking about the value to the team participants? Value to the sending local church? Value to the hosting national churches? Value to the missionaries? Or are we talking about the value to the people who ultimately receive the ministry?

The answers to each of these questions could be widely different. A short-term team might have great value to the team members and yet be of little value to the people who ultimately receive the ministry. This does not necessarily negate the value of the short-term project, but it does tell us that we need to do better next time. Our goal is to have high value marks with all five groups mentioned.

THE DUAL PURPOSES OF SHORT-TERM MISSIONS

Short-term missions has two primary purposes: ministry and mobilization. Short-termers can do many important ministries which can enormously benefit the ministries of the missionaries already on the field. These may include:

Preaching	Personal evangelism	Teaching
Local church work	Health care	Music
Disaster aid	Women's work	*Jesus* Film
Construction	Children's ministry	
Leadership training	Sports	
Teaching English	Children's work	

Perhaps the greater long-term benefit of short-term missions, however, lies not in the actual ministry done but in the mobilization value of the experience. Nothing more effectively arouses a lifelong interest in world missions than a short-term mission experience. Missions vision is better caught than taught.

In evaluating a short-term experience, most projects fall somewhere on a line between ministry value and mobilization value. Some projects are stronger in mobilization value and some are stronger in ministry value.

Mobilization Value————————————Ministry Value

I once led a volunteer team to assist an American missionary in an Eastern European country. Our days were spent doing door-to-door evangelism and our evenings were spent holding evangelistic meetings in a community cultural hall. All the team members had participated in prior short-term projects and already had hearts for the world. The mobilization value for this team would therefore be very low, but the project's ministry value would rate very high. They really got a lot of significant work done.

On the other hand, I also once led a team of 30 people on a mission project to a Central European country. Most were rookies on their first mission trip. They did far less strategic and significant ministry than the Eastern Europe team, but the participants came home fired up with a new vision and heart for the world. The ministry value of the team would be lower, but the mobilization value for this team would be very high.

Does this mean that the Eastern Europe team was more valuable and significant than the Central Europe team because they had a better ministry? Absolutely not! Both teams accomplished important purposes. We must beware of super-spiritually evaluating short-term missions only in terms of ministry done. Ministry and mobilization are both valid purposes for short-term teams.

We now come back to the question, What is the value of short-term missions? Let's talk about some of the reasons why you and your church should become involved in short-term missions.

GLOBALLY FOCUSED PRAYER

We all agree that we should pray for missions. But in reality, most of our churches pray very little for the world. And when we do pray, it is often without understanding and passion. Short-term involvement will revolutionize missions prayer in your life and in your church. Research studies of short-termers show that they dramatically increase their prayer for global concerns following their trip. A short-term experience helps to put faces to our prayers. It helps us to better understand what to pray for. It helps us to be more motivated to pray because we now recognize both the urgency and the need.

GIVING

Researchers have had a field day studying the relationship between going and giving. A STEM Int'l Ministries study found that short-term participants on the average doubled their missions giving as a result of their short-term experience. James Cecil's doctoral study found that 70 percent of the short-term volunteers surveyed increased their missions giving as a result of their volunteer experience. Tommy G. Purvis's research project found that 76 percent of the volunteers reported increased missions giving as the result of their volunteer mission trip.

My own doctoral research project came up with similar results. Over three-fourths of the respondents reported increased missions giving as a result of their short-term mission experience. When asked why they were giving more, over half of the people mentioned the word *need* in their answers. They all said the same thing—although in different words. They are now giving more to global missions because the short-term experience allowed them to personally see the needs.

Personal was another common word used. People said that they were now giving more to global missions because the trip helped to make missions personal to them.

Dan Ray conducted a study of all Southern Baptist churches from South Carolina who participated in partnership missions projects between 1989 and 1992. The average South Carolina Southern Baptist church increased giving during this time to the denomination's Cooperative Program by 2.77 percent. Those churches, however, that participated in partnership mission trips during this period increased its giving to the denomination's Cooperative Program by 16.16 percent. When people personally see the needs, they are more motivated to give.

VOCATIONAL MISSIONARIES

There is a direct relationship between short-term missions and long-term vocational missionary recruitment. From my trips, I have found that at least one person or couple on each short-term team sensed a call to vocational missions or had a call confirmed as a result of the trip. I was once told that 7 out of the 21 Southern Baptist missionaries in Romania first came to Romania on a short-term trip.

Several doctoral studies have explored this link between short-term missions and long-term vocational mission calling. Perhaps the most important was done by Herman Russell. He studied International Mission Board missionary appointees and found that over 75 percent of them had some type of prior short-term mission experience. Furthermore, he found that the short-term mission experience helped the vast majority of the potential missionaries to determine God's call and helped them to be more desirous of going into missionary service.

> "If we want long-term missionaries, we have to be committed to short-term missions."—Scott Olson

In *The Missionary Call*, Ronald A. Iwasko surveyed 192 missionary candidates and veteran missionaries serving with the Assemblies of God. They were given a list of 24 potential factors and asked to indicate on a level of one to nine the influence each factor had on them as they considered vocational missions. Six of the top ten factors that influenced them to become missionaries involved some kind of face-to-face exposure with foreign culture—often through a short-term mission experience.

Conclusion? The short-termer stream has been the single greatest pipeline for flooding the world with new long-term missionary recruits.

REVIVAL

Writer/speaker Henry Blackaby once said, "Revival will come to the United States as volunteers come home." Short-term projects are catalysts for both personal and local church spiritual awakening. Reaching outward helps both churches and individuals to change inwardly. Selfless giving helps us to get our eyes off our own problems and to focus on helping others.

A short-term experience helps people to grow spiritually. One pastor shared that his trip resulted in "a renewal in my own heart—a rekindling of remembering what is important—to present Christ and not get so caught up in church politics and selfishness here in the United States." Tommy G. Purvis's study, "Partnership in Crosscultural Mission," actually documents how short-term projects help people to grow spiritually.

> "Church-to-church partnership most often releases awakening and revival into a church, releasing people for witness at home and abroad."—James Glynn

DISCIPLESHIP

Short-term experiences present unprecedented discipleship and ministry training opportunities. Jesus Christ used short-term mission projects in order to train His own disciples in ministry (Mark 6:7). The training and preparation phase of a short-term project provides an opportunity for the team leader to require the participant to take ministry training, submit to accountability, and to develop disciplines in prayer, Scripture memory, and Bible study. Many of the participants would never be motivated to do this without the pretrip requirements. This is why a short-term project offers unprecedented discipleship opportunities. The wise team leader will take full advantage of this. I'll come back to this in the chapter on preparation and training.

One common criticism of short-term missions is that people go overseas to do what they will not do here at home. But we must realize that often the overseas experience provides the discipleship channel and motivation to help them to begin doing what they ought to do. One man told me, "It is a crying shame that God had to send me 5,000 miles away to show me what I should be doing here at home."

> "God is far more interested in you having an experience with Him, than He is interested in getting a job done."—Henry Blackaby and Claude King

CHANGED LIFE AND CHANGED ATTITUDES

People will return home from a short-term trip different. It changes a person's perspective of the world. That person will never again view the world in the same way. The person discovered people to be the same all around the world with the same desires and problems. One woman confessed that she was close-minded before going. The experience helped her "to be more open and receptive to people of other countries and lifestyles." Another woman wrote that the trip gave her an "awareness of a world outside of the United States."

> "Taking part in a mission team will strengthen your faith, touch your heart, deepen your friendships, and change your life."—David Forward

One man's first impression upon arriving at his mission location was, "These people don't have anything." In a little while he admired how "they did so much with so little." Later he began to realize that "they have so much that I do not." When he got home and back to his job, he understood that "none of the things I have really matters."

I'll never forget hearing an American pastor tell an Eastern European church, "We had hoped to come and help you in some way, but you have blessed us more than we have helped you."

FRIENDSHIPS

Relationship building is another major benefit of short-term mission experiences. Team members will build lasting friendships with national believers, missionaries, and fellow team members. One national believer summed things up when he said, "God has done more than just start partnerships. He has started friendships—which is a lot more!"

If you want people to desire to go again, prioritize relationships with people—not just activity and ministry. Ask yourself, "If God called me to come back, who would I want to come back and see?" If circumstances permit, allow your people to stay in homes of believers.

ENCOURAGEMENT AND HELP

Your visit will be an enormous encouragement to those you go to work with. You'll encourage them with your excitement, enthusiasm, and new ideas. Your team can model evangelism to the missionary and national believers. They can model to national believers the commitment and capabilities of average church members. Your new ideas and new methods and help may revolutionize the work.

This new era in world missions requires that short-termers and long-termers work together as a team to do the job. Both bring important gifts to the job. It has been said that long-term missionaries bring direction and stability. Short-termers bring velocity. Both are needed.

The long-term missionary plants churches and disciples the people. The relationships and vision of the vocational missionary are essential. They are like

> "No two-week participant . . . can take the place of the truly committed, hot-hearted, full-time witness. Nor can any hot-hearted, loving dedicated missionary ever take the place of the dedicated layman and preacher who comes to share even for one week in his country. There is a tremendous need for all of us to do all we can do in God's power. To attempt the job without both missionary and lay volunteer would be to tie one arm behind our backs and say we were going to win a world without using the tools and materials God has provided."—Dub Jackson

EQUIPPED FOR ADVENTURE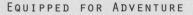

the ship's rudder—providing direction and steering the course. The short-term missionaries, however, can be like the wind in the sails. They can give thrust and velocity to the ministry. They bring resources, prayer, and tremendous enthusiasm. They can function like a global SWAT team. They can move in quickly, do the job, and then go home. One missionary told a visiting short-term team, "You have done in two weeks what it would have taken me two years to do."

The wise vocational missionary will learn how to use the energy and gifts of the visiting short-termers. This new era in world missions requires that we utilize both long-termers and short-termers—working together to spread the gospel.

THE MOST IMPORTANT REASON

There is a final reason why your church should consider sending people on short-term missions. It is the most important reason. Throughout the gospels, Jesus repeatedly told His followers to go to the nations. The same is true today as it was 2,000 years ago. We need to go because Jesus told us to do it.

> "Judge a church not by its seating capacity but by its sending capacity."—Rick Warren

PASTOR, DON'T BE AFRAID

There are some pastors who are afraid of short-term missions in their churches. Their fear is that it will drain off energy and funds needed for building up the local body and growing the church. The wise pastor, however, should never fear short-term missions. It can only help the local church. Short-termers return home to help excite their churches for missions. They help to personalize missions for the home church. They help to interpret missions to their churches with enthusiasm, realism, and personalization. They often function as mission mobilizers in the church. Their personal spiritual renewal can often be contagious. They come home as better witnesses, better givers, and better workers and leaders in their local churches. They can be a catalyst to spiritual renewal in church. Reaching outward helps churches to change inward. It can also improve your church reputation and credibility with the nonchurched community when they see your church's vision to help others. A wise pastor will create and support opportunities for his people to do global missions and will be amazed to see his audience become an army.

> "Mission teams energize the church. They instill in the congregation a healthy sense of pride in their church."—David Forward

So What Value?

And so, is short-term missions really worth the time and money invested? It really depends upon how you measure value. Most people who have gone on a short-term project, however, will answer that it was one of the greatest experiences of their lives.

One evening, volunteer Jack Hinton was leading congregational singing for a worship service at a leper colony on a Caribbean island. He asked the lepers if they had any favorite songs to request. One woman who had been strangely sitting with her back toward the pulpit turned around. Hinton said, "I saw the most hideous face I had ever seen. The woman's nose and ears were entirely gone. Her lips had almost rotted away. Then she lifted a fingerless hand in the air and asked, 'May we sing "Count Your Many Blessings"?'"

> "Make the short-term experience the centerpiece of your church's missions program."—Monroe Brewer

Jack Hinton was so overcome with emotion that he had to leave the service. A friend followed him out to encourage him. "Jack," he said, "I guess you'll never be able to sing that song again, will you?" "Oh yes, I will," replied Hinton. "But I'll never sing it the same way again." Hinton is one of thousands of short-term volunteers who have been changed by a short-term missions experience. And so, what is the value of short-term missions? Ask someone who has gone.

> The missions heart of your church will be in direct proportion to the number of people you send on short-term teams.

CHAPTER 3

CRITICISMS OF
SHORT-TERM MISSIONS

Short-term missions has received harsh criticism. Not everyone
is excited about this growing phenomenon. Some label missions
as:

- McMissions (drive-by missions)
- Hit-and-Run Missions
- The Amateurization of Missions

Some of this criticism is deserved and some undeserved. What are
some of the criticisms and how can these problems be dealt with?

"SHORT-TERMERS DEVELOP DISTORTED, LIMITED VIEWS OF MISSIONS."

Short-term experiences have the potential of giving a distorted
view of missions. It is impossible to gain a full understanding of
the complexities involved in cross-cultural ministry in a trip of a
few days or weeks. It is also possible that the short-termer may
see Christian ministry unrealistically only in terms of the glam-

our of travel to exotic places, the excitement of meeting new people, and the joy of seeing people respond readily to the gospel. It is also possible that the short-termer can arrogantly begin to consider himself an expert on missions—having easy answers to complex, tough questions.

Another problem with short-term ministry is that it usually tends to be organized in places that are either fascinating or are easily accessible—often in already evangelized areas of the world. The more difficult and needy places are usually avoided. The short-termer often does not see the unreached peoples living in Muslim, Hindu, or Buddhist countries. This could certainly give a distorted view of missions. It would be interesting to have someone research what percentage of short-term teams go to unreached 10/40 Window areas. My personal estimate is that it would only be about 2 percent because the very nature of short-term missions ministry excludes these places. Short-termers are very, very limited in what they can do in these places.

Short-termers often forget that the very nature of the short-term project excludes another critical element of missions—long-term discipleship. Volunteers need to remember that the Great Commission is not to make converts but to make disciples (Matthew 28:18–20). Discipleship requires the one element that short-termers do not have—extended time. It takes time to build trust and friendships with people of other cultures and to help them to grow in their relationship with God.

So what can we do to help give our teams a more balanced view of missions? We need to teach on this both in the pretrip training and also in the post-trip debriefing. We need to do a better job teaching our teams that their particular experience is not the whole global missions picture. It is like a snapshot compared to a video. The snapshot gives a specific scene where the video gives an overview. Short-term work is only one part of the Christian global missions movement. Also, the particular field visited is only one place in a big, big world. Short-termers need to avoid tunnel vision and focusing only on where they have been. They need to ask God to use the short-term experience as a catalyst to give them a true global focus and global heart.

"SHORT-TERMERS NEGLECT FOLLOW-UP."

It is easy to go to an area and indiscriminately give out tracts and Bibles to strangers as if they are disembodied souls. That is called hit-and-run missions. It violates the New Testament pattern of evangelism that marries the declaration of the gospel with the demonstration of the gospel. Visiting short-termers need to keep two principles in mind in order to promote adequate follow-up.

First, it is important to relate all the ministry done to a nearby local church. For instance, tracts that are given out should have the address of a recommended church in the local area. All personal evangelistic conversations ought to end with an invitation to a nearby local church. The names and addresses of interested seekers ought to be given to the pastor of the nearby church.

When a group conducts a children's backyard Bible school in an apartment commons area or park, the children should be invited to an evening Vacation Bible School at the local church. The goal is to help connect the seekers with the nearby local church. Without this, then all you've done is indiscriminate, irresponsible evangelism with no hope of follow-up of any kind.

The second principle is that both visiting short-termers and your national hosts mutually agree upon a follow-up strategy. The plan should be agreed upon in advance of the project. Visiting teams should understand that follow-up could be an immense task for the missionaries and national believers who remain behind. It is not fair for the short-termers to blitz an area and thoughtlessly leave the long-termers and national believers holding the bag. Consider leaving funds for follow-up literature and staffing to do the follow-up. Even better, the short-term team might leave behind one of their own team members to stay longer and coordinate follow-up efforts.

"SHORT-TERMERS ARE INSENSITIVE TO CULTURE AND ACTUALLY CAN DO HARM."

An African pastor once told some visiting Americans the story about an elephant and a mouse who were friends and who decided to throw a party and invite all their friends. They drank and they sang and they danced and danced and danced. Nobody had a better time dancing and celebrating than the elephant. After the party, the elephant looked for his friend, the mouse. He was horrified when he discovered the body of his friend, the mouse. Inadvertently, in his partying, the elephant had flattened his friend! "Sometimes, that is what it is like to do missions with you Americans." the African storyteller commented. "It is like dancing with an elephant."

The short-term team serving in Southern Africa had worked very hard to make the evangelistic "power bracelets." They proudly wore them and also gave them out by the hundreds— often without explaining the meaning. What they did not realize was that bracelets were seen as a way to protect people from evil spirits. One African commented, "Oh, the Americans need protection from evil spirits also!"

It is true. Short-termers are often insensitive to culture and sometime actually do harm. But the fault does not lie with the basic concept of short-term missions. The fault lies with inadequate training and orientation. The fault lies with insensitivity, cultural ignorance, and improper attitudes. These are problems that can be solved with a little work.

"SHORT-TERMERS DISTRACT CAREER MISSIONARIES."

I'll never forget my Eastern European partnership facilitator Onisimus telling me as I was unloading at the airport to come home: "Scott, I'm glad to see you come. And I'm glad to see you go!"

There is no question that short-termers can place incredible demands upon their hosts overseas. Short-term teams can create major logistical headaches for the host. Also, short-termers who have bad attitudes, those who are prima donnas, and those who are arrogant or unprepared can do serious harm. It is no wonder that some missionaries have rightly complained about short-termers.

In spite of these possible problems, a wise missionary will learn to see the long-term benefits of short-term missions. He will learn to harness the energy and gifts of the short-termers in order to help the work. If a missionary cannot see the long-term potential in a team, then it is better for the missionary to refuse the team and reject the project than to accept it out of duty.

My experience is that there are two classes of missionaries out there. Some value short-term teams and use them effectively to further the spread of the gospel. Others see short-term ministry as a waste of time, waste of money, and a interference with their important work. Younger and newer missionaries tend to value short-term teams more because they themselves are often the product of a short-term experience. Older missionaries tend to have a harder time accepting the value of short-term teams.

You can do several things to help make the short-term project more of a blessing and less of a distraction to your hosts. First, be sensitive to the time demands put upon your host. Your goal is to pack every minute and keep everybody working all the time. But be sensitive to the fact that your host already has a full plate. He must be responsible for your group ministry arrangements, transportation, housing, food, translators, and troubleshooting your problems. On top of this, he must keep his regular ministry going and also maintain home responsibilities. Hosting a short-term team can be like having guests in your home for an extended period of time. You enjoy them, but it is a lot of work. It helps a lot if you will be sensitive to the workload of your host and also appreciative of all that he does. Try to see things from the viewpoint of your host. Be slow to criticize and complain.

The second thing that you can do to help your host is to be sure that there are adequate pretrip communications. This is a must if misunderstandings are to be avoided. Communicate clearly with your host well in advance concerning logistics (housing, transportation, meals, translators), ministry, and expectations. You may even want to send a facilitator in advance of the team to help with the practical arrangements.

Thirdly, communicate a sincere interest in your field hosts. Some hosts have felt burned and used by short-term teams. One of the real tests of a short-term team is how your host privately feels about you once you return home. Would they be happy to have you back? A missionary whispered to his wife as they watched the team board the airplane to go home: "Free at last! Free at last! The volunteers are gone. I'm free at last!"

Determine that your team will be a blessing to your hosts. And don't just define *blessing* as a pat on the back as you leave. Find out ways you can really help your host. For instance, call them before the trip and ask, "What can I bring you? What can I bring your family personally and what can I bring you that will help you in your work?"

Lastly, seek to understand the ministry strategy of your host missionary and how your team can fit in and help. If the short-term team is helping to meet the priority ministry objectives of the missionary, then the missionary will be busy with the team but not distracted from his ministry. The team is contributing to his ministry. Clearly communicate to your host missionary that you are coming to serve him. Let him tell you what he needs instead of you telling him what you're going to do.

"Their motivations for coming are often wrong."

People go on short-term trips for many different reasons. Some certainly go with improper motives. Team leaders should help short-term applicants to sort through their motivations for going. Applicants need to be asked directly, "Why do you want to do this?"

In the final analysis, however, don't worry too much about motives. My experience is that God can use bad motives for good purposes. Although there are always mixed motives, surveys indicate that the vast majority of the people participate because they want to be personally involved in missions and genuinely want to share Christ and/or help the missionary.

"Short-term missions is a way to avoid long-term commitment."

This is a very serious charge. In *Run with the Vision*, a missionary in Africa asked a new missionary, "How long are you out for?" The man replied, "Well, I'm going to try it for six months and see how things work out." Another missionary caustically commented that short-termers "test the fields like someone smelling, squeezing, and sampling the fruit at the local market. If the climate, language, culture, and amenities are acceptable, then God might be leading them to extend their commitment. However, if things don't go as they hoped, then it must not be God's will for them to stay."

These are hard words, and perhaps unfair, but they need to be considered. God is calling people to full, unconditional obedience to Himself. The process of discerning God's will for our life is not as easy as most preachers make it out to be in their sermons. "Tasting and seeing" the field can be part of discerning

God's will for vocational long-term missionary service.

There are those, however, whom God is calling to vocational missions but who brush off that call and assuage their conscience by short-term service because they are unwilling to make the sacrifice necessary for long-term service. They may become short-term mission junkies who go from one part of the world to another and yet never really obey the will of God to invest their lives totally in one place overseas. Short-term missions is no substitute for long-term commitment and obedience to the will of God—wherever and whatever that may be.

> "Short-term missionaries today must see each project as one stop in a longer journey."—Bryan Slater

"BAD SHORT-TERM EXPERIENCES CAN DO MORE HARM THAN GOOD."

A poor experience can turn off an individual and poison churches to future international missions effort. The possibility of a bad missions experience always exists. On the other hand, the positive value of short-term experiences far outweighs the remote possibility of a bad experience. Fortunately, bad experiences are rare. If things do go wrong, proper debriefing is one way to turn the bad into good. The best solution, however, is to work to ensure that the short-term experience is indeed a good one.

"SHORT-TERM MISSIONS IS NOT COST-EFFECTIVE."

I hear this criticism more than any other. A missionary complained that the funds required to send a youth choir of 40 to Africa to sing for a few weeks could support 240 African evangelists for an entire year. At first glance, the criticism seems completely valid.

Unfortunately, it is not as simple as that. Those who gave to send the 40 youth to Africa would not have given the same

EQUIPPED FOR ADVENTURE

money to support 240 African evangelists. Money given to short-termers tends to be over and above what would have otherwise been given to missions.

Also, if we are going to make a cost-benefit analysis, we must consider the long-term benefits of short-term missions. For instance, consider the leader in an American church who goes on a short-term trip and then comes home and tells his home congregation, "Before, I had a head for missions. Now I have a heart for missions." How do you measure the cost/benefit of a changed life? How do you measure the increased prayer and financial support that will come for the rest of his life as the result of this experience? How do you measure the value of this person being changed from being a missions bystander to being a missions mobilizer? How do you measure the thousands of dollars that this person will give over the rest of his life to global missions causes as a result of his short-term experience? How do you measure the ripple effect that spreads throughout a church when a leader catches the vision? How do you measure long-term missionaries called out as a result of a short-term trip?

Short-term projects are expensive—especially in terms of actual ministry accomplished. But how do you measure changed lives? A short-termer recently said to me, "I realize that it (a short-term experience) is not the most efficient way monetarily. But by changing our hearts and our lives—it is the most efficient way."

CHAPTER 4

PROJECT OR PARTNERSHIP?

I mentioned earlier that the most effective short-term mission is always in the context of an ongoing, long-term partnership relationship.

The world has changed. In the past, missions was "from the West to the Rest." Missions was seen primarily as sending our white, Anglo-Saxon Protestant missionaries to the heathen overseas. Now, the epicenter of Christianity has moved from North America. More than 75 percent of evangelical Christians live outside the United States and this percentage is rising yearly. The growth of the non-Western missionary movement has turned traditional global missions topsy-turvy. In the last 25 years, non-Western missionaries went from being about 20 percent of the total protestant global missionary force to now dramatically outnumbering Western missionaries. And all this has happened in the past 35 years!

The one area where we remain the global Christian leader is in wealth. American Christians control an incredible 80 percent of the Christian wealth globally! How should this affect our funding patterns and strategies? The sad thing is that many denominations, missions agencies, and churches have completely ignored these changes and continue to budget as they did 25 years ago. We are still functioning under the old traditional "from the West to the Rest" model of missions—spending 99 percent of our missions money to send our own American missionaries to the world. Do we still have the old arrogant, colonialistic, paternalistic view that we Americans are the saviors of the world? Furthermore, 98 percent of our budgeted church moneys is spent in North America and 90 percent is spent on the local church itself or its immediate area of ministry.

It is time to wake up! It's a new day. We must quit thinking in the past. We need to rethink some things. It is time to reevaluate our foreign policy. It is a new world! We need new ways for new days!

PARTNERSHIP: A BETTER WAY

Partnership with nationals has become one of the most effective ways to do missions in the twenty-first century. Effective missions is now done in the context of strategic mission partnerships. Short-term volunteer teams are an integral part of this new partnership strategy.

Let's begin by defining *partnership*—In *Partners in the Gospel*, James Glynn defines partnership as "an association of two or more Christian autonomous bodies who have formed a trusting relationship and fulfill agreed-upon expectations by sharing complementary strengths and resources to reach their mutual goal." Partnership is summed up in the Greek word, *enosis*, which means, "to unite, to link." Note that the common goal is to advance the gospel through sharing complementary strengths. Partnership may be agency with agency, church to church, church to missionary, church to agency, etc.

The biblical model of partnership is Paul and the Philippi church. Paul calls the Philippi church his partners in ministry (Philippians 1:5). The Book of Philippians is a song of Paul celebrating their mutual partnership in ministry. Their partnership involved mutual communication, financial support (Philippians 4:15), sending of laborers to work with Paul (Philippians 2:25), mutual prayer for each other (Philippians 1:4), mutual encouragement, expression of love, and special care during crisis/suffering times (Philippians 3:10).

Partnership is attractive for several reasons. First, it models the church body doctrine. "The body is a unit, though it is made up of many parts; and though all its parts are many, they form one body. . . . Now you are the body of Christ, and each one of you is a part of it" (1 Corinthians 12:12, 27). For the first time in history, we can truly experience oneness, personal *koinonia*, mutual sharing with Christ's body on a global scale, cross-culturally through mission partnerships.

Secondly, partnership offers ownership. We can't change the whole world, but we can make a difference in one definable place. We feel that this place is ours. Partnership gives ownership and a face to our missions, instead of just supporting missions generically. It provides a personalized channel for the church to be involved in hands-on missions. It leads to the establishment of relationship.

Third, partnership releases synergy. Synergy means that two partnered can accomplish more than twice as much as two independent. And three is even better! (Ecclesiastes 4:9, 12). We can get more done for the kingdom through partnership.

VOLUNTEER TEAMS AND PARTNERSHIPS

The most effective short-term missions is in the context of a ongoing partnership relationship. Some churches go a different place every year. They are project-oriented instead of partnership-oriented. Ongoing short-term missions is an expression of an intentional, strategic partnership.

The apostle Paul began his second missionary journey by saying to Barnabas, "Let us go back and visit the brothers in all the towns where we preached the word of the Lord and see how they are doing" (Acts 15:36). Paul's method of missions was short-term repetitive deployment. He went on seven short-term missionary journeys. Each time he preached, won converts, and planted new churches. Then he made subsequent follow-up short-term trips to the same places to see how they were doing and to encourage them.

My experience is that a team's ministry effectiveness increases each time they return to the same location. First-visit teams often come relatively unprepared. Follow-up visit teams building on an established partnership come far better prepared because they know the situation, know the people, and know the needs. They are building on already-established relationships. They now have credibility and relationship with the people. They know what to expect, how to prepare, and what to do. They are more relaxed and confident and useful.

So, do we want McMissions projects, or do we want to be genuine missionary partners in the gospel? Are we interested in just making a great commotion, or do we truly want to help fulfill the

> Paul's mission trips "were not one-shot efforts. He sought to maintain significant contact with those to whom he ministered. He loved them, prayed for them, sent them letters, and sought to encourage them. This does not seem to be the case in most short term missions today. . . . One must question whether true relationships are developed and nurtured as we see in Paul's pattern."—Bryan Slater

Great Commission? Is our goal to offer entertaining new trips to our church, or to make a significant missions impact? Are we interested in projects or partnership?

How to Get Started: Identifying and Choosing a Partner

1. Prayer. Partnership must begin with prayer—prayer for guidance and wisdom. "Help, God! What should we do?"

2. Attitude. There should be self-examination at the beginning of this process. What is our attitude? Are we approaching this new experience as a learner and a servant? Are we prideful and arrogant?

3. Priorities. What is our church's mission strategy and priority? What are we looking for in a partner?

4. Relationship. What relationships do we already have with missionaries and/or particular fields? Where has God already gone before in our church to create interest?

5. Assistance. Sometimes you need help to find a partner—a "MissionsMatch.com." How do you find this? Many missions agencies can help you with this.

6. Person. Although you may be partnered with a ministry, a church, or an organization, the key to that partnership is the point person that you will relate to. Do you connect with this person? Does he speak your language? Do you have common goals, doctrines, and ministry philosophies? Is this an approved, respected person in the partner church or organization? Does he have a hidden, personal agenda?

7. Communication. Can you easily communicate internationally with this prospective partner by email and/or telephone? You can't partner if you can't communicate!

8. Personalization impact. Will this partnership capture the imagination of your church? Is it something your people can get excited about and support? Prior relationship makes this much easier.

9. Patience. Think long-term! It often takes time for a true partnership to gel and come together. Be patient.

Structuring and Defining the Partnership

Structuring and defining the partnership must be done mutually with your partner. It cannot be done properly by phone or email. It is best done personally. There needs to be a lot of talking, a lot of genuine listening, and a lot of note taking. Here are the issues that need to be dealt with:

1. Discern the field partner's vision and needs. What do they want to do and how do they need help? Your role here is to listen, ask questions, and understand. It is improper for you to impose your vision and agenda on them. Our motto should be, Their Vision Is Our Focus.

2. Purpose. What are we trying to accomplish through this partnership? What is our purpose? Of course the broad goal is to advance the gospel through sharing complementary strengths. But how do we do this. Talk about specifics. Put some flesh on the skeleton.

Now that you understand their vision and needs, how can you help? Talk about possibilities. Also, what do you need and want out of this partnership? Talk honestly about mutual roles, involvement, and responsibilities. A partnership should be reciprocal. Both sides should benefit. This leads to our next point.

3. Reciprocity. Unhealthy partnership occurs when you have a one-way flow of assistance—whether it be money, personnel, or ministry. True partnership is coming together for mutual benefit. It is characterized by mutual hospitality, love, prayer, healing, sharing of information, sharing of material gifts, modeling, discipleship, sharing hope and encouragement, and friendship.

4. Volunteer teams. What is their role in this partnership? How often will you send teams? How are they needed? How many people?

5. Communication. Without direct communication, there can be no partnership. Exchange phone numbers, addresses, email addresses, and fax numbers. How often will you communicate? Without regular communication, the partnership will languish. Who is responsible for communicating? Information and communication fuels partnership.

6. Length of partnership. How long are we committing ourselves to each other? It is best to set a time and extend if necessary instead of leaving it open-ended. A good beginning might be three to five years.

7. Financial investment priorities. One important aspect of a partnership is sharing financial resources. Remember that American Christians control 80 percent of all Christian wealth globally. We can't be good stewards and ignore our financial role.

What are their financial needs and priorities? Discuss together and itemize the priority of the things that they need help with. However, be careful making promises. Also, keep in mind the twin dangers of partnership and dependency—discussed later in this chapter.

8. Accountability and reporting. Accountability is the open, voluntary sharing of information—especially financial

> "Western Christians also need desperately to experience the living faith, love, and sacrifice of two-thirds of the world's Christians. We need the injection of spiritual vitality from their witness to us, which pales to anything physical or material we might offer them."—James Glynn

information. Accountability is an essential key to successful partnership. Two big questions arise: How does one have accountability in a cross-cultural partnership without controlling? Secondly, how does one have accountability without implying mistrust?

Realize that many cultures don't have the same attitudes towards accountability and reporting that we do in the West. In *African Friends and Money Matters*, David Maranz states that in many African cultures "social harmony is a highly valued goal. . . . Questioning the handling of money and other resources will inevitably lead to tensions and the disruptions of surface harmony. . . . Such unpleasantness is to be avoided if at all possible. . . . Precision is to be avoided in accounting as it shows the lack of a generous spirit."

The Westerner, however, believes that accountability and reporting in financial matters is essential in order to ensure honestly. Laxity in accountability can foster temptation, which may lead to corruption. Accountability is our concession to our sin nature. We believe that accountability does not imply mistrust, but it does help maintain trust. It is difficult to trust someone who is unwilling to be accountable.

In spite of cultural differences, accountability is essential to successful partnership. Both partners must have honest discussions on this subject at the very beginning of the partnership negotiations. In order for the partnership to work, there must be a common commitment to accountability.

9. Empowerment instead of dependency. How may the partnership empower the partners to excel more instead of creating an unhealthy and paralyzing dependency that stifles local incentive? These things must be discussed up front between the partners. This is a giant issue that the next section covers.

10. Leadership. Who are the leaders on both sides who are responsible? Who are the point people? Who is responsible

for communications, keeping the vision before the people, and seeing that whatever you have agreed upon is carried out? On the American side, it is best that the pastor not take this role. He should delegate.

11. Memo of agreement. It is a good thing to write out and document what you have agreed upon. This is not a contract. It is simply a memo of agreement between two partners/friends. Our memories grow poor over time.

12. Formal acceptance. The memo of agreement should be reviewed by all the parties involved and formally voted upon. This may include the American church board, the church congregation, the overseas partner board, and the overseas church (if the partnership is with a church).

PARTNERSHIP AND DEPENDENCY

Sharing resources is an essential part of partnership. But how do you share resources without creating an unhealthy dependency? How do you empower instead of creating a paralyzing passivity that stifles local incentive?

After 14 years of organizing mission partnerships, I regularly hear people who throw out the feared D word (*dependency*) to prove that one should never share resources with nationals. They teach, "Sharing resources is always a slippery slope that creates unhealthy dependency." Self-sufficiency is the absolute value. Many of these people are only spouting outdated, unevaluated mission policies and have never really wrestled with the issues involved or with the changing global situation.

There are two extremes involved in this issue of dependency and the sharing of resources. One extreme is not to share resources with nationals. The other extreme is to throw money at them without any accountability or plan. One extreme is to say that you will not help because help will cause dependency.

The other extreme is to help without any concern of dependency. One extreme withholds funds because of the fear of creating unhealthy dependency. The other extreme withholds accountability because of the fear that if we attach task/strategy/accounting demands to our gifts, then we are exercising paternalistic control. One extreme provides help with no funding. The other extreme provides funding, often with no help. And sometimes, the giving partner is simply too lazy, too uninterested, or too ignorant of the issues and problems.

Share no resources with nationals.	Give money with no accountability.
No help due to fear of dependency.	No concern at all of dependency problem.
Give help with no funding.	Give funding (often) with no help.

Please note that there is an excluded middle here. Does it have to be either/or instead of both/and? My experience is that usually balance is found in the middle, not on the extreme. My plea is that we reach a balanced view on this—that we exercise some common sense. Partnership and mission always has risks. Ministry is never "clean," whether it is in the local church or on the mission field. There will always be problems, misunderstandings, and abuse at times. But let's not throw the baby out with the bath water!

"Is it non-Christian to give aid in the name of Christ to specific, urgent benevolence needs?"

Sometimes it seems easier to take an inflexible position instead of being willing to wrestle with the problems. The truth on this issue of financially assisting national works is found in the middle. There is a tension between generosity and responsibility In *Building Strategic Relationships*, Daniel Rickett believes that "those who would share resources in the work of the gospel must learn to navigate between the need to care for others, and the need to care for themselves."

We should help, but we should help with wisdom, common sense, thought, study, discussion, and prayer. Some things are just common sense, and yet it is amazing how naive many of us are. For instance, don't fund your partner 100 percent. Don't send money to individuals. Don't give without a plan or accounting. Daniel Rickett shares perhaps the most important questions to consider when helping: "Have we contributed to the self-developing capabilities of our partners? Are we helping to build their capacity or are we simply relieving their needs?" We should help in a way that empowers instead of stifles local initiative.

DEPENDENCY IS NOT A BAD WORD

Dependency is not necessarily a bad thing. Webster's dictionary defines *dependent* as "relying on another for support." Jesus told the itinerant workers that He sent out in Matthew 10 to be dependent upon others. Later, Jesus sent out His Twelve on a short-term mission adventure. He told them to take nothing for their journey—no bag, no staff, no bread, no money, and not even an extra set of clothes (Luke 9:3). Why? Because He wanted them to learn to depend on God to provide their needs through other people. And that lesson of learning to depend on God to provide through others was just as important as the actual ministry work they were going to do.

The Bible celebrates dependency in the body of Christ. We are a body with different parts and each part is dependent upon the other (1 Corinthians 12). We are told to carry one another's burdens (Galatians 6:2). If we see our brother in need and have the means to help, we should do so (1 John 3:16–20). Paul collected funds from the Asian churches to help the suffering church in Jerusalem (1 Corinthians 16:1–3).

Most of us in ministry are dependent financially. Pastors are dependent upon church members to give. Missionaries are dependent upon donors. Denominational employees are dependent upon donor churches. We are all dependent on funds from other sources to help support our ministry. So what is wrong when a national worker is dependent upon funds from an American source for his or her ministry? Is the money somehow corrupted when it goes overseas? *Dependency* does not have to be an ugly word.

UNHEALTHY DEPENDENCY

There are two kinds of dependency: healthy and unhealthy. What makes dependency healthy or unhealthy? Dependency is not a bad thing. Permanent dependency is the bad thing. Unhealthy dependency occurs when outside assistance encourages passivity and stifles local incentive and responsibility to support their own. "We don't need to give because the Americans are paying for it."

In a wonderful booklet entitled, "Freedom and Dependency in Christian Partnerships," Alex Araujo lists eight evidences of unhealthy financial dependency.

> "If the giver can give without the need for control, and if the receiver can receive without being stifled, financial dependency ceases to be a problem."—Alex Araujo

1. Are local believers being prevented from learning to give sacrificially?
2. Is the ministry failing to increase its income level from local/national sources?
3. Is the ministry losing creditability because of foreign funding?
4. Is the ministry's goal setting and decision making unduly influenced by foreign funding sources?
5. Is foreign funding stunting the development of indigenous parachurch structures?
6. Is the foreign funding agency unwillingly assuming moral responsibility for personal care of workers, such as their medical and retirement needs?
7. Does the ministry leader have exaggerated power and authority because he has access to foreign funds?
8. Is worker support level set by outside funding sources rather than by the worker's peers?

OTHER MINEFIELDS TO AVOID

Partnership is risky business. Anything worthwhile in life has risks. Dependency is certainly the greatest risk associated with strategic mission partnerships. But there are several other problem areas that you need to be alert to.

1. Paternalism. Next to dependency, paternalism is the greatest danger. This means that one partner is trying to control things—including the decision-making process. The golden

rule is that those who have the gold make the rules. However, when this happens, healthy partnership is torpedoed. Here is some good advice for the partner with the gold.

- Don't define goals and methods unilaterally.
- Don't base the relationship on a one-way flow of resources.
- Don't allow money to become the most highly valued resource.
- Don't fund the full cost of a project without clear justification.
- Don't interfere in the administration of the partner's organization.
- Don't do for others what they can better do for themselves.

2. Forgotten purpose. Over time, it is easy to forget the original vision of the partnership. The partnership becomes an end to itself, instead of the means to the goal. The partnership itself is not the goal. It is the means to accomplish a common purpose and goal. What is that goal? Work hard to keep it a purpose-driven partnership.

3. Misunderstandings and conflicts due to cultural differences. Never underestimate cultural differences. Never assume that you think alike. Communicating with your mission partner may sometimes be like communicating with your mate—except magnified several times more. Communication issues are giant in partnerships. And they are made worse by the fact that you are usually forced to communicate by email or phone internationally instead of face-to-face.

What's the solution? Relationship! Focus on personal relationship with your partner. Spend lots of personal time together. Focus on understanding yourself and understanding your partner. Become a student of his life and culture. You cannot settle for an impersonal business relationship.

This is very difficult to do—given the nature of international partnerships. Your partner doesn't live around the corner. You can't take him to lunch once a week. You can't pick up the phone and call him just any time and talk about anything. The best solution is to encourage great humility, sensitivity, and prayer.

4. One size fits all. "Thank you, I don't need help or advice. I know what I am doing. We've always done it this way. This is the way we did it in Haiti and we'll do it this way in Romania. We have our policies (written 30 years ago) and we'll do it by the book!"

These attitudes have their roots in arrogance and pride. Arrogance means that we think that we know all the answers and understand all of our problems and their solutions. It means that we don't need advice or input because we already have it all figured out. The result is that the leader is never growing, never learning, and never changing.

> "The illiterate of the 21st century will not be those who cannot read and write, but those who cannot learn, unlearn, and relearn."— Futurist Alvin Toffler

Individuals, church mission committees, and denominations make this mistake often. The longer people are in positions of leadership, the more susceptible they are to this. In *Change Is Like a Slinky*, Hans Finzel describes this. "We naturally think we become experts by virtue of longevity. Yet a common effect of all those years of practice is an isolation and conformity to traditions. We end up with the answers to questions people quit asking long ago."

Humility means that we do not have all the answers. We may not even know the right questions to ask. Does my ministry reflect humility? You know what insight is, but do you know what outsight is? Outsight is input from those outside your group or organization or decision-making team. The arrogant have no need for outsight. The humble welcome it. Are your doors open to criticism, new ideas, and information? How well do you listen?

5. Insensitivity to crisis times. The test of true friendship is the time of crisis—the time of trouble. Churches, organizations, and individuals all go through periods of crisis. Where is the partner when he is needed most? Where is the "fellowship of suffering"? A good partner's antenna is tuned to these hard times. Are you just a fair-weather friend, or will you be there to help and encourage during the rough times?

6. Relationship neglect. Many American partners only define their partnership in terms of sending a check and periodically sending a short-term volunteer team. But there is no regular communication and relationship maintained. If you don't talk to your mate, you have no relationship. The key to relationship is communication. Again, Paul's relationship with the Philippi church is the model for partnership. There was mutual love, prayer, letters, visits, and encouragement.

A Brother Like That

A man came out of a store and saw a young boy hanging around his new car. Suspicious of the boy, the man asked, "What are you doing?" The boy replied, "Admiring your car." The man and the boy talked a while about the car. The boy seemed fascinated with the car and asked all sorts of questions. Finally, the boy asked, "How much does a car like this cost?" "I don't know," the man replied. "My brother gave it to me." "Wow!" the boy replied. "I wish . . ." "That you had a brother like that!" interrupted the man. "No sir. I wish I could be a brother like that!" A mission partner has that privilege.

CHAPTER 5

Getting Started

OK, you're sold on doing a short-term project. Where do you begin? How do you get started? Here is an overview of the process. We'll work through these different elements in the succeeding chapters.

1. Choose the project.
2. Plan the trip.
3. Establish cost and a plan to fund the project.
4. Promote the project.
5. Recruit your team.
6. Prepare the team.
7. Do the project.
8. Follow up on the project and the team members.

How to Choose a Project

It's a big world out there. The needs and opportunities are endless. How do you choose where to go and what to do? Choosing the right project is absolutely essential to successful short-term missions. As you choose, think about three key words: *relationship*, *partnership*, and *project*.

RELATIONSHIP

How do you pick a project? Or a global location to work? Or a missionary or a missions organization to work with? Do you just open the phone book and look up "missions" or "short-term missions"? You wouldn't do that even if you could find those things in your phone book. Why? Because you don't know anything about those people or organizations.

So how do you choose? You look for people or organizations that you do know and trust. The most important word in choosing a project is the word *relationship*. Look for relationships that God has already established between your church and other missionaries, missions organizations, or nationals. Look for ways where God has already gone before to create interest.

Are there any missionaries from your church serving overseas? Are there any missions organizations closely related to your church? Are there any parts of the world that your church is especially interested in? Churches respond best to projects where they feel some kind of ownership and with whom they can bond. They prefer to work with people they already know. This means that we should look for already-existing ties within our church with the missionaries and missions organizations. Missionaries out of your church, or supported by your church, should be your first priority for short-term involvement. Missions organizations that are closely connected with your church should be your first choice. If possible, work with people you already know, love, and trust. Build on those relationships that God has already begun.

> Three Key Words:
> *Relationship, Partnership,*
> and *Project*

PARTNERSHIP

The first important word was *relationship*. The second most important word is *partnership*. Many churches mistakenly use the shotgun approach to short-term missions. Each year they work at a different location. The most effective short-term missions, however, is always done in the context of developing long-term, ongoing partnership relationships. Consider adopting projects where your church can have long-term, ongoing strategic partnership relationships. Look for projects where your church can become financially, prayerfully, and also personally involved. Look for projects that have strategic value and can capture the imagination of your church. Go into the partnership not thinking single project, but ongoing partnership relationship. Consider returning several times and building upon the ministry and relationships that you have established. It is OK to do new projects, but consider maintaining relationships and partnerships with past projects also.

NEED?

Is this project only something that you personally want to do or is it really needed? Why is it needed? What is the value of the project? Does it strengthen the work of the missionary? Does it stimulate and not suffocate local initiative? Does it make a real contribution? Is it doable? Beware of choosing a project based upon sentimental reasons instead of strategic value. Look for ways to increase the strategic value of your projects.

One of the neglected fields for short-term missions is among the unreached peoples of the world. Sixty-one percent of all short-term projects are in Latin America—where there are already thousands of churches and millions of believers. This does not negate the value and importance of projects in already evangelized fields, but more emphasis needs to be on unreached areas.

Pioneer, less-reached areas are certainly much more difficult to work in. There are good reasons why most people choose Latin America. These reasons include easy access, low cost to get there, adequate translators, adequate accommodations, and receptiveness to the gospel. There are also good reasons why short-term teams tend to neglect unreached areas. These reasons include the high cost to get there, shortage of structures to work through, serious hindrances to evangelism and Christian work, unreceptiveness, harsh climate, and uncomfortable conditions. These are all very important factors to take into consideration.

I am not saying that you should ignore Latin America and concentrate on sending teams only to Mongolia or the Sahara Desert, but unreached areas should become part of your local church short-term mission strategy. Short-term missions in unreached areas will certainly require more creativity—but it is doable. You will need some help from missions organizations who work in these areas, however. It is not a good idea just to show up with your team at the airport in Beijing and start handing out gospel tracts. The mobilization value of short-term missions in the 10/40 Window unreached areas generally will be higher than the ministry value.

Not only should you address the issue of whether the ministry is needed, but you should also address the issue of whether the ministry is wanted. A friend once said that the golden rule of short-term missions is to only go where you're invited. Let the missionaries or missions organizations know you are available to come, but opportunities are best initiated from the field.

Help?

The people that you work with will be critical to the success of the project. When we talk about who are we going to work with, we are basically talking at two levels—both here and on the field. First, who are you going to work with here at home to set up the project? Some large churches may have the personnel, resources, and contacts to generate and organize projects wholly in-house. Most individuals and churches, however, need the services of some agency or organization that is sponsoring and organizing the project and is experienced in short-term missions. If this is your first mission project, choose an agency to help you.

How do you choose such an organization? Sometimes it may seem like Russian roulette. *The Short-Term Missions Boom* and *The Short-Term Mission Handbook* list scores of missions agencies who do short-term missions (see appendix 1). Or, you may decide to use an appropriate agency of your denomination. In choosing an agency, however, it is best to work with someone you know or someone who has been recommended to you as competent. Ask the leadership at nearby churches that are successfully involved in short-term missions. Local church team organizers need to realize their accountability to their church and fellow team members to provide a high quality experience led by people who know what they are doing.

Work with someone who can give you and your team personalized attention. Do they promptly return your phone calls and answer your questions? Administrative negligence at the beginning should be an immediate red flag. Are they willing to personalize and tailor the project to your own team strengths and interests, or do they try to force you into their mold? Work with someone who has experience, a good track record, and good references. Check their references. Is their motivation to serve Christ or is it to make money off of you? Do they genuinely want to serve you, or do they make you feel that they are doing you a favor? Do they have a clear short-term strategy and philosophy? Can they help you train and prepare your team? Do they have the field structure overseas to actually pull it off? Keep in mind that different agencies are strong in different areas.

Not only is it important who you work with here at home, it is also important who the field people are you will be working with overseas. Who is going to organize all the details on the field? Who is organizing the actual ministry and schedule? Who is organizing local transportation, housing, meals, and translators? This may be either a national church leader or a missionary. The success of your project, however, depends upon this person.

> Success and Failure Are in the Details.

Whenever you talk with a sponsoring ministry organization, you must find out who is going to do the detail setup on the field. There is significant value to actually taking a scouting visit to the field to scope things out and talk things over with the person on the field.

MINISTRY PROJECT DEFINITION?

Most ministry teams fall into one of three types:

Exposure Teams. The primary purpose is exposure to the needs. Ministry may not even be possible if it is closed country. Prayerwalking is one type of exposure team.

Ministry Teams. These teams do actual ministry such as evangelism, discipleship, local church ministry, and children's work.

Service Teams. These are involved in support ministry such as construction, health care, mercy ministry, renovation, and relief ministries. These teams are good for members who are intimidated by up-front ministry or evangelism.

What is the specific ministry that you are going to do? What are you trying to accomplish? What is your purpose? Every project should have a clearly defined purpose. Does this project fit with the giftedness of your people? Is it true missions? Missions may involve benevolence work, but benevolence work does not necessarily involve the Great Commission.

Research shows that the prime motivation for people going on short-term trips is to be personally involved in missions work and to help the missionary. People want to have a hands-on experience in the work. People are interested in people. Recently, a church sent a construction team to Africa to help build a church. The project was designed so that the Americans worked by themselves almost all the time on the construction project with little or no exposure to the Africans. After a few days, they were very unhappy campers. An essential element of their project was missing. They wanted to do more than just lay bricks. They wanted to work with the African people and to share with them. Construction always needs to be mixed with evangelism and events that will allow relationships and bonding with the local people.

> Three Types of Teams: Exposure Teams, Ministry Teams, and Service Teams

Missions agencies involved in short-term work must take note that people are most interested in helping the missionary and evangelism. Agencies must structure their projects with this in mind if they want to attract people and churches to participate in their programs.

PERSONALIZATION IMPACT?

It is important to choose projects that will most effectively personalize missions to your people—both to team members and to the church at large. Remember the dual purposes of short-term missions—ministry and mobilization. Will this project help turn on your people to the world? Does it excite them and capture their imagination? Does it offer opportunities and channels for a large number of the people in your church to be personally involved in the project through giving, praying, or going? Does the actual project allow for people with different skills and abilities to participate? Our goal is to involve as many people as possible.

Is God in This?

Lastly, is there a sense that the hand of God is initiating this project and drawing us into this? This is certainly a highly subjective criteria for choosing a project, but it is very important. Paul had such an experience when a man from Macedonia appeared to him in a vision and said, "Come over to Macedonia and help us" (Acts 16:9).

You probably won't have a vision from heaven, but there should be a sense that God is in this. The whole process of choosing a project should be bathed in prayer in order to discern the mind of the Lord. Also, your pastor and your church missions leadership team should be supportive of this project.

Sometimes the directing hand of the Lord may seemingly violate some of the criteria which we have suggested for choosing a project. That's OK. We must yield to God the right to direct in seemingly unusual directions. Philip is a good example of this principle. Philip was having a very successful missionary ministry in Samaria (Acts 8) when suddenly an angel of the Lord sent him to the desert. What an odd thing! Who was Philip going to evangelize in the desert? But God brought Philip from his successful ministry in Samaria to evangelize one special person in the desert. And this one special convert became the means of first introducing the gospel to the entire continent of Africa! The foolishness of God is wiser than men (1 Corinthians 1:25).

> The most effective short-term mission will always be in the context of an ongoing, long-term partnership relationship.

CHAPTER 6

PLANNING, PROMOTION, AND RECRUITING

Before you can promote the project and recruit your team, you must be able to give them general details about the project. Planning project logistics is a process. General details must be determined up front. Specific logistical detail planning can wait for later. For instance, they must know the departure date up front, but they do not yet need to know how they will get to the airport. General details now. Specifics later.

Preliminary Planning Checklist

Where? Location and with whom?

When? Project dates? How many days?
Calendaring considerations? School schedule? Holidays? Workdays away? Seasons of year? Weather?

Who? Kind of people you are looking for? Ministry skills? Age issues? Students? How many people do you need? Nonchurch members permitted?

How much? Cost? How much do you need to charge? (Here you must create a preliminary budget, based on air travel, land travel, insurance, lodging, meals, visas, translators, etc). Deadlines? What financial deadlines must you require? (These are affected most by buying air tickets and deposits required.) What other ministry project expenses do you anticipate and how will they be paid for?

What? What kind of ministry do you intend to do? (List possibilities here).

How? Funding plan? Visa/passport issues? Team training/meeting schedule? Logistical arrangements (those necessary now; many can wait till later).

"Leave your nets and follow Me."—Jesus

WHEN DO I GET STARTED?

When do I need to begin the planning process? How much time do I need? How early should I get started? Here is a simple plan.

Eight to five months from departure: Approval/ Planning/ Promotion/Recruiting

Four to two months from departure: Fund-raising

Four months to departure: Training and team preparation

If you wait too late to promote the project, then people will not have time to arrange their schedules and be able to raise necessary funds. Plan well in advance!

PROMOTING A SHORT-TERM PROJECT IN YOUR CHURCH

Your goal is to encourage people to move from the pew to the plane. Many churches find that the same people always go on mission trips, and are unsuccessful in persuading new people to go. Here are some suggestions that might help you promote the project and encourage people to go.

1. Identify key people that you would like to see go. Gather them together for a formal meeting (perhaps at your home) to share your vision, get their input, and challenge them to participate. We often wait for volunteers, but the Acts 13:1–3 model is different. Specific people were asked to go on mission by the church leaders. Discuss with the volunteers the names of other potential members. Assign core group people the job of personally contacting those others discussed.

2. Create a quality brochure giving all details: cost, dates, deadlines, project description, giftedness of people needed, project schedule, description of ministry location, and what to do if you are interested.

> "If you give people the same information seven times in seven different ways, then they get it!"

3. Promote the project in all church bulletins and publications. Include the time of first information meeting scheduled. Run these for several weeks. Be creative. Use artwork, written testimonies, and photos to draw attention to the project. Bulletin inserts are great.

4. Promote the project in worship services. This is especially powerful if the pastor does it. Consider a slide and video presentation before or during a service. Promote the project in several consecutive services because you usually only have about one-third of your congregation on any given Sunday. Do it a different way each time. You might have a veteran short-termer share how the experience changed his life. Just be sure to give him a firm time limit!

5. Consider organizing a live phone call with the people overseas that you will work with and patch it through the loudspeaker system so that all can hear. Have your overseas host officially invite your church to come and work.

6. The most effective recruiting is letting people recruit people. Give those who are excited about going some brochures and assign them the task of recruiting two others. People are more apt to go if they have friends who are going.

7. Realize that people attract people. "This sounds interesting, but who is going?" If they don't know anyone who is going, then they are hesitant to sign up. Advertise names of those already signed up.

8. Visit Sunday School classes and small groups. Give a two-to-three-minute promo presentation, explain the project, leave brochures, announce the time of the first information meeting, and ask for prayer.

9. Hold an information meeting. Don't call it a mission trip information meeting. Call it something less daunting—such as [*Country Name*] Mission Trip Q & A Time. Consider holding two identical meetings over several weeks so that people may have more than one opportunity to attend. The team leader/organizer should personally follow up with a phone call and email those who attend or show an interest.

10. It helps enormously if the pastor is going. His participation gives credibility to the project. If the pastor is willing to go, then it must be important!

11. Have an information table in a prominent area of church manned before and after services—with brochures and a display. Delegate to team members the job of designing and manning this table.

> **Information Meeting Agenda**
> ___ Obtain names, phones, and email addresses of attendees.
> ___ Give out brochures and application forms.
> ___ Discuss project plan/ministry details.
> ___ Discuss dates and travel plans.
> ___ Discuss cost and fund-raising plan.
> ___ Explain why they are needed.
> ___ Emphasize passport/deposit deadlines.
> ___ Passports.
> ___ Question-and-answer time.

THE FOUR BIG QUESTIONS

It is essential that you address the questions, fears, and excuses of potential team members. There are four big questions that most people will have.

> **Four Big Questions**
> 1. How am I needed?
> 2. How can I pay for it?
> 3. Is it safe?
> 4. How can I find time?

What can I do? How am I needed? How can I help? People must see that they are needed, can make a contribution, and are qualified to do something needful on the team.

I can't afford this. How can I pay for it? Most people can't afford a mission trip. You must assure them of a viable plan to procure the funds. I'll address these issues in next chapter on funding your project.

Is it safe? In a post-9/11 world, many people have serious concerns about the safety of air travel and their security in another country. You must address these concerns. Review appendix 2, "Is It Safe to Go on a Mission Trip?"

I don't have time to go. How can I find time to do this? Explain that if God calls, God will provide. Also explain the concept of tithing time. We tithe our money. Are we willing to tithe our time?

Seven Great Excuses for Not Going

1. "We don't have the money." (Mark 6:37-44)
2. "I can't get off from work." (Matthew 9:9)
3. "I can't leave my family." (Luke 9:57-62)
4. "Lord, I can't speak well." (Exodus 4:10-12)
5. "The timing is not right." (Haggai 2:1)
6. "Someone else could do it better." (Exodus 4:13)
7. "Lord, I just don't want to go." (Jonah 1)

FEAR FACTOR

In order to move people from the pew to the plane, not only do you have to answer the four big questions, but you also have to address their unexpressed fears. Fear of flying. Fear of failure. Fear of the unknown. Fear about the food. Health fears.

Excuses are often the expression of unexpressed fears. In Exodus 4, Moses gave God a whole list of excuses why he couldn't lead the children of Israel out of Egypt. But the real, unspoken issue was fear. You must help people work through their fears.

APPLICATION

Use an application form to gather the information needed to select and screen potential team members. Application forms should give the following information: full name (as appears on passport), address, phone numbers (work and home), email address, birth date, passport information, employment information, health concerns, emergency contact name/number, ministry experience, and health insurance information including beneficiary. Check out appendix 3 for a sample application form.

HINT: Create a group mailing list for your mission team to keep everybody informed.

If you do not know the person, request a written personal testimony and a reference from his or her pastor, church staff member, or small group/Sunday School leader.

SCREENING AND SELECTION

You must decide whether everybody is welcome or whether you are going to screen the applicants. The team organizer always faces this tension. You want the people to participate, but you don't want the wrong people to participate.

However, one bad apple can ruin the whole barrel. A short-term project involves an enormous investment of time, energy, and money. People are going to be thrown together as a team into stressful, strange, cross-cultural situations where they will be dead-tired and sleep-deprived. A serious health, emotional, or relational problem can utterly consume the energy of the group that needs to be focused on accomplishing the particular ministry project. Some individual health problem can ruin the entire project for everyone involved. One church had a project where a young single woman had a complete nervous breakdown and had to be sent back to the United States. It is absolutely imperative, therefore, that some effort be made to screen the applicants.

Team leaders need to be alert for disruptive personalities—people who are going to create stress, disunity, and confusion during the project.

Screening may be done on basis of written applications, references, personal interviews, and reputation of the individual in the church. Take information given by references seriously. Press references to be wholly honest with you. Difficult and stressful situations could have been avoided if a missions pastor had been honest with me when contacted for a reference. Be alert to red flags and follow your gut feelings.

Ten Selection Issues

Potential team members need to be screened on the basis of ten things.

1. Sense of call. Why do they believe God wants them to do this?
2. Gifts and abilities that can contribute to the team and to the project.
3. Attitudes. Are they willing to listen, to serve, and to complete any trip preparation requirements placed upon them? Do they exhibit attitudes of servanthood, flexibility, selflessness, cooperativeness, sensitivity, and respect for authority? Do they have a heart to work, or are they just looking for a free paid vacation?
4. Relationships. How well do they get along with others? Disruptive people?
5. Health. Are they physically healthy? What is the emotional health?
6. Spiritual condition. I purposefully used this word instead of spiritual maturity. A short-term project is wonderful for a young Christian. It is important, however, that all participants be genuine Christians and have a true heart to walk in holiness and obedience to Christ.
7. Moral issues. Applicants need to be screened concerning moral issues that could compromise the ministry and testimony of the whole team. These issues might include substance abuse, alcohol, sexual immorality, etc. Some teams require participants to sign a team covenant. See appendix 4 for a sample covenant.

8. Age issues. How old must a team member be in order to go? Do you have an upper age limit? Older people need to be screened especially in terms of health and flexibility.
9. Team size restraints. How many people can go?
10. Church membership. Will you allow people from other churches to be part of your team?

PRAY FOR HELP

Trust God to help you in the recruiting process. If He has led you to organize this team, then He will call and raise up these people. Trust God in the screening process. Jesus Christ spent the entire night in prayer before He chose His disciples (Luke 6). God will honor your prayer for wisdom if you will only ask. It is not unusual to feel a little overwhelmed as you begin this short-term mission adventure. God will help you!

> "One of the significant challenges for the church during the next decade will be to get those families with children at home to become involved in missions."—Vicki Tanin, Jim Hill, and Ray Howard

CHAPTER 7

FUNDING YOUR PROJECT

A friend shared this experience: "I was invited to accompany a man on a mission trip to South Africa. He shared the cost with me and in my heart I thought, 'That is too expensive.' I was interested in going and even dropped a hint at a missions committee meeting. One of the committee members advised that I plan to go and trust God for the money. I didn't want to impose on anyone for the funding and I began to realize that I couldn't afford to go, so I did not pursue it. I did not share my desire to go with anyone. I didn't even really pray about it because it just seemed to be out of reach.

"Several years later my wife and I responded to God's call to missions as a career. After seeking to go to Angola, we ended up in South Africa. I realize now that God wanted to give me a head start in South Africa by inviting me to go years earlier. I didn't trust Him or trust my fellow brothers and sisters. I should have trusted God and stepped out in faith."

Your project will cost a lot of money. Most people cannot afford to pay for a mission trip out of pocket. Like my friend, the high cost of a short-term mission trip can often frighten away

> If you are trying to put together a team, and you do not teach them how to raise their funds, then your group will probably fail to come together.

prospective participants. This need not be. My purpose in this chapter is to help give you confidence to trust God to provide the funds and to offer some ways to fund your project.

It is the team leader's job to help your team mobilize their funds. If you are trying to put together a team, and you do not teach them how to raise their funds, then your group will probably fail to come together.

Is God calling you?

The first question to consider is not How much does it cost? or Can I afford it? The first question to consider is not How can I get off work? or Can I get out of school? The first question to consider is whether God is calling you to do this. Does God want you to go on this trip? You must settle this question first before you ever begin worrying about the cost, getting off work, getting out of school, or getting someone to keep the kids. Is God calling you to do this?

> "God is able! When He says go, you do not need to see how. Just be obedient."—Bruce and Michelle Steffes

Like my friend in the story, some people decide at the very beginning that they cannot afford the cost and so dismiss the idea of going without ever even praying. This sort of thinking is "checkbook guidance." Checkbook guidance is the method of determining the will of God by how much money you have in your checkbook. The reasoning is very simple: "If I can personally afford the trip, then I'll go. If I can't afford it, then I won't go." What's wrong with this thinking? If every Christian endeavor was determined by the amount of present available funds, little would ever be accomplished for the kingdom. Where is God in this process? Where is faith in this process?

Several years ago I had the opportunity to go on a short-term project to Africa and made a fatal mistake. I decided that I would go if God provided the money. There was no money provided and I did not go. I learned a hard lesson. My problem was that I approached the short-term opportunity all wrong and depended on checkbook guidance. I never really wrestled with the issue of God's calling. What should I have done differently? I should have first settled the issue of God's calling. And if God was calling me, then I should have launched forth in faith with the attitude, "I'm going and I will trust God to provide."

Many others made the same mistake. "I'll go if God provides the money." Guess what? Most of these people never went. Many others, however, approached the opportunity with a different attitude. "I believe God is calling me and I'm going no matter what!" Anyone who approaches a short-term opportunity with this attitude will never go.

There is a very important spiritual principle operating here. Where God guides, God provides. This is why the most important issue is not how much it will cost. The first and most important issue is whether or not God wants you to do this. If God wants you to do this, then He will be your provider and helper. You must launch forth in faith trusting Him to provide. God will never call someone to do something without providing the resources for it. To go or not to go is a faith issue, not a financial issue.

FOUR SOURCES OF PROJECT FUNDS

Where does the money come from? Four sources:

> **Four Sources of Project Funds**
> · Personal funds
> · Church funds
> · Fund-raisers
> · Support letters

1. Some people pay all or part of their way out of their own pockets. There is nothing wrong with this. However, if this were the only way, then only those who are financially well off could go on mission trips. Even if you can afford the entire cost, there are some great advantages to asking others to help. Be careful that you

are not robbing someone else of a blessing by not allowing them to help. Also, is there a lesson about humility and dependence upon God that you need to learn. Bruce Steffes says, "Sometimes God really does want you to pay for your trip entirely by yourself. But . . . sometimes paying for everything yourself is just an excuse to cover your pride and embarrassment at asking."

2. Mission projects are often fully or partially funded from the church mission budget or from special church offerings. The church leadership determines these disbursements and/or church missions committee or mission policies. Here are some common practices:

Percentage. The church might normally grant a certain percentage of the cost—anywhere from 10 percent to 100 percent. The disadvantage of fully funding the mission team from the missions budget is that it limits the number of people who can go, and can quickly deplete the church missions budget.

A set amount. The church might give all team members, regardless of the cost, a certain predetermined set amount. For instance, each person going on a trip gets a $400 grant.

Scholarship according to need. My church, for instance, will consider granting scholarships for the balance needed after team members have first sent out a prescribed number of support letters in a timely manner.

First-timer scholarship. Set a scholarship percentage or flat amount for first-time short-termers.

Special offerings. Some churches may choose to permit a special offering for the mission team. This may be in a particular church service or ongoing through the use of envelopes in the church pews. These funds may be divided equally between team members, disbursed according to need, or go to buy team supplies.

<u>Pastor and church staff</u>. Some churches don't feel comfortable with their leaders asking for personal support to go on a mission trip. Pastors and church staff are often funded directly from the church missions budget, or from another church budget source.

3. A third source of funds for mission projects is through fund-raisers. These fall into basically three categories:

<u>Sell things</u>: Flowers, wrapping paper, pumpkins, discount coupon books, doughnuts, yard sale items. Holiday-related sales are effective.

<u>Sell services</u>: Babysitting, housework, yard work, general house maintenance, car washes, etc.

<u>Sell food</u>: Bake sale, men's cake bake, spaghetti dinner, romantic formal dinner, pancake breakfast, chili or barbeque cookoff, dinner with your mission destination theme.

One of the most effective things is to have a Sunday mission team day. In the morning service, team members should give testimonies, and a special offering for the team should be taken. Then there should be a fund-raising lunch immediately following the morning service (spaghetti? barbeque?). Bake sale goods and other sale items should be available at the lunch location. Students may have a table set up where they sell certificates for an evening's babysitting or a half day of yard work.

4. The fourth source of funds is to ask others to help through support letters. This is the most effective and most common source for mission project funding. It involves others in praying and giving and encourages a missionary vision in the body of Christ.

Fund-Raising Ideas
Men's cake bake/auction
Spaghetti lunch
Formal dinner
Pancake breakfast
Chili/barbeque cookoff
Car wash
Babysitting
Yard work
Yard sale
Bake sale
Sell flowers for Mother's Day
Sell Christmas wrapping paper
Pumpkins for fall
Entertainment coupon book
Doughnuts
Craft fair

Building a Partnership Team

As we consider how to raise the personal funds for a short-term project, we need to review what is the purpose of short-term missions. Do you remember? Short-term missions has two primary purposes: ministry and mobilization. One of the goals of a short-term mission project is to mobilize people to become involved in missions. If you go alone to the mission field, then you alone are impacted through the experience. But if you can mobilize a support team to stand with you in prayer and financial support, then you involve and influence far more people for global missions.

The goal, therefore, is to involve as many people as possible in the short-term mission experience. This is best accomplished by gathering together a support team who will pray for you and help pay the way financially. These people are more than just supporters. They are partners.

When an entire team goes from a single church, then a short-term mission project is a wonderful way to involve the whole church in the support process and thus significantly raise the entire church's awareness, interest, and involvement in global missions. Work to make this a whole-church project—not just a group of Lone Ranger short-termers doing their own thing.

It is essential that you see this mission project as a team effort. I have read that there are eight support personnel for every one person on the front line in an army. The front-line soldier could not accomplish his task without the support personnel standing behind him. This is also true in short-term missions. You may be the front-line soldier, but you cannot accomplish your task without a support team standing behind you praying and paying. You are not the only one participating in this trip. You are the representative of all the people who send you. They are just as much a part of the team as you are (see 1 Samuel 30, especially vv. 24, 25). You must, therefore cultivate a team mentality. If you do not really see them as part of your team, and value them as your sending team, then they will not feel a part of your team. It is imperative that you work on making them feel that they are valued partners in the ministry.

William Carey is known as the father of the modern missions movement. As he prepared to go to India, he told his friends, "I will go, but you at home must hold the ropes." God's plan is that you have a team of people holding the ropes. These people will pray for us, encourage us, and some will help us financially.

Perhaps you think you can do this mission trip on your own—depending on no one but yourself. Bad idea! The success of your work over there depends upon your partners here! Perhaps you can afford to pay for the trip without help. How much better it is to have a team of people behind you who are a part of what you are doing. You involve more people, interest more people, and mobilize more people to participate in missions when you recruit partners.

Beggars?

Having a support team means that others will help pay your way. Some people feel very uncomfortable with the idea of asking others to help support their short-term mission financially. They see it as begging. This is, however, an unbiblical perspective. Support raising is not rattling a tin cup for spiritual welfare. God's plan is that we are to help and support those who are serving Him in ministry. We are stewards of all that we own and are called to invest these resources in God's work. Support raising is simply looking for God's chosen avenue to provide for what God has asked you to do.

In Luke 9:3, Jesus sent out the Twelve on a short-

"How, then, can they call on the one they have not believed in? And how can they believe in the one of whom they have not heard? And how can they hear without someone preaching to them? And how can they preach unless they are sent?" (Romans 10:14–15).

term mission adventure. Amazingly, He told them to take nothing for their journey! No bag. No staff. No bread. No money. Not even an extra set of clothes! Why? Jesus wanted them to learn to depend on God to provide for their needs through other people. And that lesson was just as important as the actual work they were going to do.

Trusting God to provide for our needs through others grows our faith. We are forced to trust God to provide. Many short-termers say that the fund-raising process was really more exciting than the actual ministry project because they saw God supply so miraculously.

A Partnership Team Plan

Six-Step Partnership Plan
- Make a list.
- Write a letter.
- Mail.
- Pray.
- Record responses.
- Communicate.

Step 1: Prayerfully prepare a list of 50 to100 names of people who might be interested in partnering with you on this project. Remember, 50, not 5!!! It is OK to send letters to non-Christians. A former stripper saved at my church once sent a letter to her old boss, the club owner. He gave $1,000 for the trip and later prayed to receive Christ when she went back to give her report after the project.

Organize your partnership list with multiple columns for name, address, phone numbers, first letter sent, follow-up contact, gift received, thank-you note sent, postcard sent from the field, post-trip report sent, and gift sent. This list will help you keep up administratively with communications to your support team members (see appendix 5 for a sample prayer/financial partnership record).

Do not be misled into thinking that people are not interested. You will be amazed how interested they are in what you are doing—even if they are unable to help you. People may not be interested in giving their hard-earned money to vague missions budgets with the hope that it will somehow be used somewhere to accomplish something. But they are very interested in giving to support mission work by people that they know personally. People will give to people they know.

Step 2: Write a letter and tell them about the mission opportunity (see sample letter in appendix 6). Keep the following things in mind as your write your letter:

- One page only!!! Remember KISS—keep it short and simple.
- Tell where you are going, why, and what you will be doing.
- Make it as personal as possible—not a form letter.
- Include project dates.
- Include cost and deadline for the funds needed.
- Personally sign each letter.
- Share prayer needs.
- Give instructions concerning any gifts:
    Where to send
    Who to make the check out to
    Tax deductible
    Your name should not be written on the check.

Step 3: Mail your letters. These should be mailed at least six weeks before you need your funds—preferably earlier. You are actually mailing three things.

- Your letter
- A self-addressed stamped envelope
- A response card (see appendix 7)

Step 4: Pray.

Who to write?

Family
Friends
Parents of friends
Parents' friends
Pastor
Sunday School teacher
People you work with
Other churches nearby
Civic clubs
Your physician and eye doctor
Your dentist
Coaches
Your bank
Church members
Sunday School classes
Family attorney
Your insurance agent
Neighbors
Senior citizen club
Former/present teachers
Church missions committee
Business leaders
Exercise class

Step 5: Record all responses and gifts on your partnership record (see appendix 5).

Acknowledge all responses immediately with a thank-you. They deserve it, and your mother would be proud of you!

Step 6: Communicate. Those who commit to give and/or pray become your partnership team. Treat them as valued team members and communicate with them regularly. How would you feel if you invested in a mutual fund and received no information about your investment? Remember, you want them praying for you. Their gifts are helpful, but their prayers are essential. Consider giving them a wrist rubber band or plastic hospital bracelet to wear to remind them to pray while you are gone. Other ideas include a trip prayer calendar and a prayer card that you can easily create on your computer.

Call them right before your departure and share any last-minute prayer needs. Perhaps send a postcard and/or email from the mission field. You will be amazed how much a card will mean to them. (In order to do this, you must remember to take their postal addresses/email addresses with you on your project.)

When you arrive home, send a personal thank-you note and a trip report to your support team members, or go visit them personally. A letter should detail what happened on the project and how it affected you.

There is nothing more discouraging than to support a person on a mission project and then never hear from that person again. Remember, you could not have gone without their support. They are your partners. Also, by sharing your experiences with your partnership support team, you continue to spread the vision for global missions. You will discover too that these supporters will be much more likely to help you the next time you want to go on a short-term mission project. If you take care of the people who take care of you, then you will find that they will help take care of you the next time.

Lastly, you might want to pick up small thank-you souvenir gifts overseas to bring home to your partnership team members. Gift ideas include coins or small currency from the country you visited, a small flag, postage stamps, maps, letter opener, postcards, or a calendar from that country. Deliver these gifts in person, if possible, or with a personal note if a visit is not possible. This is a wonderful way to let your partnership team members know how much you appreciate and value them.

CHURCH ACCOUNTING AND TAX ISSUES

It is not unspiritual to consider the tax issue. Wise stewardship of God's money is eminently spiritual. Volunteer short-term mission trip expenses can be considered as tax-deductible charitable contributions (IRS Publication 526, 2005 edition). This is true even if you are giving your own funds towards your own mission project.

People must give to your project through your church or through the sponsoring nonprofit IRS 501(c)(3) organization. The name of the individual who is to be sponsored should not be on the check.

If you are leading a church team, it is best to channel all contributions through your church office. You can work out accounting/record-keeping procedures with your church financial secretary. Often, churches will establish a designated account for these kinds of projects. Many teams appoint a team treasurer to manage the records and relate to the church financial office.

Never forget that the color of money is not green. It is red. People can get very angry over financial issues. Therefore be very careful in all you do. Funds should always go for what they were given for. All gifts should be receipted in a timely manner. There are a couple of sticky issues, however, that you will face.

What happens if someone raises more money than he needs? This question needs to be answered and communicated at the very beginning before people start raising their funds. Possibilities include putting it in the team pot to help other team members, spending it on supplies for the team, returning it to the church missions budget, or escrowing it for a future mission trip by the person it was given for. Nonprofit tax rules prevent the church or nonprofit organization from returning excess gifts to the donor.

What happens if someone does not raise enough? This is easy. Either the church gives the person a "scholarship," or they don't go. However, don't buy the plane ticket until you know what you are going to do with this issue!

What happens to the money if someone can't go? The same principles apply as if you had raised too much. Either put it in the team pot to help other team members, spend it on supplies for the team, put it in the general missions budget, or escrow it for a future mission trip by the person it was given for. The money cannot be returned to the donors.

DEADLINES

You must set payment deadlines for team members. The biggest factor in determining deadlines is airline ticket purchase deadlines. Some churches require a small deposit up front with the application. The next deadline might be a couple of weeks before tickets must be bought. The final balance is due a couple of weeks before departure. If people are raising their funds, then it is best to give them as much time as possible, and not push them too much with early deadlines. Some churches and organizations penalize people who miss deadlines—by perhaps $100. This threat often pushes people to meet deadlines. (We must take into account the sin/procrastination nature of man.)

Some churches spread out a multiple payment schedule over a several-month period, instead of just requiring one or two large payments. The positive thing about this method is that it requires people to become committed up front and helps them budget their payments over a period of time. This works well if the participant is responsible to pay for the entire trip out of his own pocket.

It is a problem, however, if the participant intends to raise funds from others for the trip. Either he must send out his fund-raising letters six to eight months in advance, or he must pay the first few payments out of his own pocket until fund-raising letters are sent out and funds begin to come it. Fund-raising letters sent six months in advance are not nearly as effective as letters sent three months in advance. There is no urgency. Also, if the participant pays the first few payments out of his own pocket, and then donations come in to cover the whole cost of the trip, legally the church cannot refund the money he has paid out of his own pocket.

> "I have been able to stand before people . . . and assure them that if God leads them to participate, He will provide all they need when they need it. Their abilities or financial status have nothing to do with what He can do."—Dub Jackson

GOD OUR PROVIDER

Part of the short-term mission adventure is seeing God provide the finances. You will discover that God may provide the funds for the trip in many different ways. You may be able to pay the entire amount out of your own pocket or you may have to trust Him to provide the entire amount from other sources. Either way, we must always remember that God is the ultimate source for all our needs. He is our provider.

> When a proposed team fails to come together, the reason is almost always a leadership problem. Other reasons may be given—lack of interest, lack of funds—but the real reason is usually lack of leadership. The team leader/organizer has procrastinated and not adequately promoted, communicated with, and helped the team to raise their funds.

CHAPTER 8

TEAM PREPARATION

Team preparation begins with leadership. Proper preparation will not happen unless someone intentionally makes it happen. Someone must be in charge and make things happen. Someone must have the vision, motivation, time, and energy to make it happen. The team will fail without leadership.

Team leader, get your people ready! That's your job! Take charge. Make it happen! Find out what you are supposed to do and get your people prepared to do it spiritually, culturally, and professionally. Avoid procrastination. Committees cannot lead mission teams.

A second essential element in team preparation is team communication. The good news is that email has made this so easy! Get everyone's email address at the first meeting and create a email mailing list group. You can give weekly reminders, prayer requests, information updates, team meeting information, and resources to the whole team in a touch of a key.

> Six-Fold Preparation
> Personal
> Partnership team
> Logistical
> Ministry activities
> Cultural
> Team building

The third essential element in team preparation is team meetings. You cannot just get off the airplane and ask your national host, "What do you want me to do?" Team meetings are essential to successful mission projects because they provide ministry training, motivation, team building and bonding, personal accountability, and necessary project information. You set your team up to fail if you do not meet. The purpose of the meetings is to prepare the team to go. Up front, team members should understand that these meetings are not optional. If they cannot participate in the preparation process, then they should not go. The meetings and preparation process are wonderful opportunities for some serious discipleship training, ministry training, and accountability that many would not submit to in other circumstances. I suggest six to eight meetings over a three-or-four month period. A half-day Saturday training period is also helpful. It is helpful to go ahead and calendar the meeting dates at the very beginning (see appendix 8 for a sample meeting schedule).

> Your success there will be directly proportionate to your preparation and prayer here.

Your meetings (and the homework you give them to do) should prepare them in six areas: cultural preparation, personal preparation, logistical preparation, ministry preparation, partnership team preparation, and team-building preparation. Let's talk about these six areas.

> "Often short-term team leaders are primarily focused on what needs to be done rather than developing people. . . . Your training philosophy should be one of a disciple maker, not simply a task preparer."—Larry Ragan

PERSONAL PREPARATION

The team leader and meetings should help the participant prepare himself spiritually, intellectually, and physically for the project. Here is a possible fitness program.

1. Reading and study assignments. This may include reading or Internet study/search on the country, people, politics, religion, history, geography, lan-

guage, and culture. Participants may also read appropriate missions biographies and encyclopedia articles or other books on missions. Don't forget to check out Patrick Johnstone's *Operation World*, the classic prayer guide on the needs of every country of the world. Great missions books can be easily ordered online at www.christianbook.com. Team members may be assigned to bring reports to the main team based upon their reading or research.

2. Devotional assignments. Appendix 9 is a 30-day Bible reading program that will help prepare team members. Use this during the 30 days preceding your departure date.

3. Journaling assignments. Begin keeping a journal 30 days before departure, during the entire trip, and at least two weeks after the project. Write down what you are learning in your Bible reading, prayertimes, and experiences.

4. Prayer assignments. Encourage the team member to create a prayer list and use it daily. Participants should pray about personal attitudes and expectations, relationships with other team members, logistics, travel safety, health issues, and ministry effectiveness. Check out appendix 10 for a sample prayer guide.

5. Letter to God. Give each team member some paper and an envelope. Have them write a letter to God expressing what they hope to see God do in and through them on the trip. Then ask them to put the letter in an envelope, seal it, write their home address on the envelope, and give it to you (the leader). Three to six months after the trip, mail the letter back to them.

6. Health preparation. The team member not only should prepare his soul, but he also needs to prepare his body physically for the project. This may include an exercise program, required vaccinations, adequate rest, and a vitamin regimen. He should do whatever is necessary to prepare himself physically to successfully accomplish the project.

Partnership Team Preparation

One of your most important jobs as team leader is to help your team members put together a group of people who will pray for them and help financially support them on this project. You will need to teach them how to do this and then hold them accountable to stay on schedule. They will need constant encouragement in this process. Teach them the plan from the preceding chapter for raising the funds. Use the team meetings to check on the progress of each person. Have they created a list of names? How many? Have they mailed out their letters? Do they need to turn in support envelopes? Help your team with the administrative details.

However, it is very easy for the team to get focused on just raising the money and forget what they need far more—prayer support. They need prayer far more than they need money.

International missions is a war. Missionaries often are invading territory held by the enemy of souls for centuries. Satan does not meekly give up his prey. The short-term missionary may experience a degree of spiritual warfare that he has never dealt with before. A spiritual battle must be fought with spiritual weapons (2 Corinthians 10:4). God has given us prayer as our most effective spiritual weapon. The true success or failure of our work will depend upon prayer.

Prayer preparation must operate at two different levels. First, there must be the team member's own personal spiritual preparation through prayer. The team leader must help the team members to prioritize prayer in their trip preparation.

Not only should there be personal spiritual preparation through prayer, but the team and team members absolutely require intercessory prayer from others to prepare the way for the team and to empower the team as they actually minister.

A prayer support team functions much as Moses did for Joshua and the armies of Israel as they battled the Amalekites at Rephidim (Exodus 17:8–13). The army of Israel was victorious in the valley as long as Moses held up his hands in prayer on the mountain. Israel won the battle that day because they had a secret weapon. The battle was not won in the valley but on the mountain in prayer. The success of our mission over there depends upon our praying over here. We only do religious work instead of genuine spiritual ministry when we fail to pray. We could see multiplied results if we could see multiplied prayer.

Help your team members to recruit a team of people who will pray for them every day. Are the team members communicating with their prayer supporters and telling them prayer needs? Once a girl asked the prayer meeting to "pray for me as I go on a mission trip to Moldova." An older woman interrupted, "And don't forget to pray for our Sunday School class also. We are going to Pigeon Forge."

Also, consider appointing a team member to be the prayer liaison to your local church. The role of the prayer liaison is to mobilize the broader corporate body of the church to remember the team in prayer.

LOGISTICAL PREPARATION

Preparing a team to go involves a multitude of administrative and logistical details. You job as team leader is to see that these things are done and done on time! Leader, plan your work and then work your plan. Make a list. Chapter 10 is devoted entirely to logistical matters. However, here are some things to get you started.

- Passport application
- Visa application
- Housing, transportation, meals
- Airplane tickets
- Team supplies
- Financial issues
- Packing list and plan
- Insurance, medical release forms, liability release forms
- Health-care issues (immunizations, health, hygiene)
- Airport transport
- Team policies (cancellation, dating, smoking, photos, begging, etc)

MINISTRY PREPARATION

Ministry preparation must begin by first knowing clearly what sort of ministry you are expected to do on your short-term project. It is imperative that the team leader get as detailed a picture as possible. Having said this, you can be sure that things will not be exactly as you expect. You will end up doing things you didn't come prepared to do and not doing everything you thought you would do. Also, always come prepared with ministry materials to do more than you expect.

Secondly, inventory and evaluate the individual and collective talents, gifts, skills, passions, and professional experience of your team. Make assignments to team members. Who is responsible to do what? Each team member should be responsible for an area of ministry—youth, children, preaching, women, or music. Other team members will assist in these areas, but there should be a team member who is the lead person in each of these areas. This lead person is responsible to gather and prepare materials, and make that particular ministry happen.

Once you know the details of your particular ministry, the team must be trained for the work they will be doing. It is wrong to invest all the money and time in a short-term project only to show up unprepared to do the work expected of you because you did not train. Appendix 11 lists several resources and ideas for working with women, youth, children, speaking in public schools, preaching, prayerwalking, Christian arts, health-care ministry, etc.

You should prepare, but you should also be prepared to do the unexpected! Imagine that you are a repair person called to fix something at a house. However, you don't know what you have to fix until you get there. What do you do? You bring your toolbox with multiple tools that will allow you to handle most any repair you find when you arrive. That is the way you must approach a short-term mission trip. We can communicate with the field and prepare our team; but when you arrive, things will not be as you expected. Count on this! You will be asked to do many unexpected things and you must be prepared and flexible. So come with your toolbox full. Your team should be multitask prepared (i.e., sermons, lessons for men, lessons for women, children's stories, crafts, music, youth work, games, testimonies, prepared to do personal evangelism, etc.).

Team training should always include learning how to develop and share your personal testimony. A personal testimony is one of the most powerful evangelistic tools. Once team members prepare their testimonies, they need to share these testimonies with the group and be critiqued. If possible, testimonies should be typed, translated into the language you are working in, and several hundred copies printed to be available to give out (see appendix 12 for a testimony preparation work sheet). Some teams require participants to have three different testimonies:

- Salvation testimony: How I Became a Christian
- Life lessons: The Most Important Lessons God Has Taught Me

- Godly passions: The Issues God Has Shaped Me to Care About Most

All team members should know how to share the gospel one-on-one and how to lead a person to Christ. As leader, your job is to be sure they know how to do this and teach them a plan if necessary. Many teams use tools such as gospel tracts, gospel bracelets, wordless book, and EvangeCubes (www.evangecube.org). Divide into pairs and practice on each other during the meetings.

Also, much of your ministry may be speaking through an interpreter. I call them interrupters! Most people have never done this before, so you should teach your people how (see appendix 13, "Hints for Speaking Through a Translator").

Most ministries will require some tools, supplies, or literature. You need to gather together all the materials necessary. If ministry materials, such as Bibles, gospel tracts, or New Testaments, are needed for your team in large numbers and in the national language, then you need to make preparation to see that they will be waiting on your team when you arrive.

Be sure, however, that your literature is culturally relevant. I picked up a tract in Romania entitled, "Baseball's Greatest Hitters." It related the steps of salvation to first base, second base, third base, and home plate. It is a well-done gospel tract. The only problem is that baseball is an unknown game in Romania.

Cultural Preparation

We had arrived in Africa the day before and now were sitting around the dinner table getting to know the leaders of the African church we had come to work with. I happened to be sitting at a table of mostly women and was working hard to meet and get to know these sisters in Christ. I worked hard to learn their names and purposefully call them by their first name.

However, about halfway through the meal, the oldest woman sweetly rebuked me in front of the whole table. "Men do not address women by their personal name." I wanted to climb under the table and hide! I didn't understand their culture.

Many Americans do not understand the concept of culture because we live isolated from the world and it's varying cultures. For some, the only cross-cultural experience they have had is going to a Chinese or Mexican restaurant.

Culture is a shared connection that a group of people have that includes language, history, belief systems and presuppositions, priorities, customs, traditions, social structures, and norms. There is a cultural difference between my suburban, mostly Anglo community and an inner-city, mostly African American community. There are cultural differences between generations. My son and I live in different cultures. But the cultural differences are most dramatic when we go to other places in the world.

For instance, in Fiji conversing with another person with your arms crossed is a sign of respect where in West Africa it implies condescension. In Singapore it is rude to leave food on your plate, but in Egypt it is rude not to leave food on your plate. In Bulgaria, nodding your head as we do for yes actually means no. Shaking your head as we do for no means yes. In Muslim and Hindu cultures the left hand is considered unclean. You never touch anyone or eat with that hand—even if you are left-handed. In Russia and the Middle East, one should refrain from crossing his legs and showing his shoe soles. It is a sign of disrespect.

Also, you are not only dealing with a different national culture, but you also must deal with the church culture that you will be working with. They will have certain cultural expressions of their faith that are very dear to them. For instance, in Eastern European church culture:

Men and women sit on separate sides of the church.

Women do not wear makeup or jewelry.

Everyone stands to pray.

Women cannot stand in the pulpit.

It is unhealthy to open windows no matter how hot it is.

Scripture should be read before the message.

Married women wear head coverings.

Do not wear the cross.

Women do not wear pants.

The preacher wears a coat and tie no matter how hot it is.

Sing traditional hymns, not contemporary choruses.

No clapping in the church (or chewing gum!).

Speakers do not put their hands in their pockets.

Culture, however, is not static. It changes over time and through exposure to other cultures and information. Because we are experiencing the greatest information and travel explosion in world history, culture is changing far faster than ever before. The things mentioned about Eastern European church culture are good examples. Things are changing in the cities where churches are exposed to Western television and visitors from the West. The young people are beginning to copy the Western practices, but the older people are holding to the old traditions. However, in the remote villages with no TV, almost all of these things are still the practice.

> "Two common reactions are seen on short-term trips. The first is typified by comments that over-idealize the national people; the second is typified by comments that are over-critical. Neither is correct."— Bruce and Michelle Steffes

Why is it so important for your team to understand, honor, and respect culture? Because insensitivity and ignorance can hinder the effectiveness and witness of your team. How? Here are three ways:

1. It helps your team to avoid offenses, conflicts, and misunderstandings with the nationals. For instance, in Asian and

African cultures, conflict situations are handled so that no one loses face. Our American confrontational approach may really blow things up. American teams tend to be project- and task-oriented. "We are spending all this money and time to come here. We've got to make things happen now!" But what if the culture you are working in is people-oriented instead of project-oriented? What if projects, program schedules, and getting the job done are just not as important as people and relationships? Other cultures have different priorities and expressions of hospitality, mealtimes, privacy, dress, greetings, family relationships, decision-making processes, role and treatment of women, etc. Can you see the possibilities of offenses and conflicts if you go into their culture not understanding these things? Attitudes of humility, graciousness, and servanthood can lessen the impact of your cultural goofs, but there is still no excuse for not trying to understand the culture.

2. Insensitivity to the culture can hinder the receptivity to the message you are bringing. The apostle Paul understood that he could more effectively express his witness if he was sensitive to culture. He spoke to Jews and Gentiles differently. He preached differently in Jerusalem than he did in Athens. Effectively proclaiming the message is more important than insisting on your own cultural way.

Sensitivity to a culture means that we are willing to voluntary give up freedoms that might hinder the receptivity to our message. For instance, women in Romanian churches do not wear makeup or jewelry. Challenge the women on your team to voluntarily

> "To the Jews I became like a Jew, to win the Jews. . . . To those not having the law I became like one not having the law . . . so as to win those not having the law. To the weak I became weak, to win the weak. I have become all things to all men so that by all possible means I might save some" (1 Corinthians 9:20–22).

> "Culture shock can start when members first see the teeming masses fighting for every millimeter of sidewalk space during Hong Kong's rush hour, smell the stench of the backstreet alleys of Cairo, or spot abandoned eight-year-olds living in the sewers of Columbia. Culture shock also occurs when we miss what we have taken for granted: no hot water for showers, the sanitary conditions of cooking facilities, the frustration of not being able to understand—nor being understood."—David Forward

give up their freedom to wear makeup and jewelry. The apostle Paul teaches in 1 Corinthians 8 and 9 that love is willing to give up freedoms if they are a stumbling block to others.

3. Understanding the culture beforehand lessens the possible impact of culture shock. Culture shock refers to feelings of personal stress, confusion, uncertainty, anxiety, irritability, and possibly depression and withdrawal that may affect people exposed to an alien culture. It does not affect everyone, but it does affect some. The longer the trip, the greater the possibility of this problem occurring. The best remedy for culture shock is prior warning and preparation so that one is not blindsided.

You can culturally prepare your team by teaching them four things:

1. Respect cultural diversity. Different is not bad. Different is not wrong. Different is just . . . different. Warn them against attitudes of superiority. Warn them to avoid criticisms and comparisons, especially in front of nationals.
   - "Back home, we . . ."
   - "Don't any of these people use deodorant?"
   - "Can you believe that outhouse!"
   - "Somebody ought to explain to these people that bathing daily is a godly trait."
   - "I wish I could bring my teenager here for a few days and let her see just how bad other people have it."

Warn them against cultural/national biases and stereotypes. "The poor are poor because they are stupid and lazy." "All Latin

Americans are lazy." "All Muslims are terrorists." "All French are arrogant and rude." Did you know that other countries often see all Americans as selfish, self-centered, wasteful, aggressive, arrogant, loud, obnoxious, immoral, and dominating? Yourteam needs to work to show other people that we are caring, sensitive, loving Christians—here only to serve and help. Vicki Tanin, Jim Hill, and Ray Howard challenge believers in this way: "Celebrate the differences. God made them! The variety of peoples, ways of doing things, foods, dress, manners, etc., are all wonderful expressions of God's creativity."[7]

2. Learn the cultural rules. The rules are different in each different culture. Some rules work in almost any culture:

> "We have done something terrible. God created us in His image, but we have decided to return the favor, and we have created a God who is in our image. He comes across as a white Anglo-Saxon Protestant Republican."—Tony Campolo

- Always greet people.
- Never shout at people in anger.
- Never make fun of people and their culture.
- Never disrespect people in front of their peers.
- Careful, careful in opposite-sex relationships.

Research the country and culture in the library and on the Internet. Perhaps assign different team members to bring reports on history, climate, social structures, politics, religion, geography, and customs/traditions. What are the cultural "no-no's"? Consider inviting someone from that country to talk to your group. You may find people by calling local universities and local ethnic churches. If possible, as a group visit a restaurant and also a local church of that culture. Rent a travel video.

Some Web Culture/Country Search Sites
www.countrywatch.com
www.odci.gov/cia/publications/factbook/docs/profileguide.html
www.peoplegroups.org
http://freedomhouse.org/religion
www.loc.gov/rr/international/spguides.html
www.aolsvc.worldbook.aol.com/wb/Browse
www.ipl.org/kidspace/browse/owd0000

3. Learn some of their language. Most mission teams work in lands where

English is not the primary language. Teams should learn a few simple words and phrases in the heart language of the people. It is amazing how important this is and how dramatically it increases your credibility among the people (see appendix 14, "Words and Phrases You Should Learn"). Even it you don't know the language, you will find that you can communicate. Try the "point-and-grunt" method!!

4. Be prepared for the differences and inconveniences. We are not on vacation!

Accommodations. Beds may be on the floor. Mattresses may be saggy or very hard. Do we need to carry spray for bedbugs? Hot water may not be available. Daily baths may not be possible. Drink bottled water only. Toilets may be outdoors.

Food. Your hosts will give you the best they have. Turning up your nose at it will cause hurt feelings. However, if something looks or smells really bad, you may politely refuse it. Remember the missionary creed: "Where He leads me I will follow. What they feed me I will swallow."

> "Our views on health and cleanliness, our obsession with time and punctuality, and our passion about financial accountability put us in conflict with much of the world."—Bruce and Michelle Steffes

Schedules. The rest of the world is not as time-conscious as Americans. Meetings will start when people get there. Transportation and meals often will be late arriving. Follow the lead of your host and stay relaxed. No one is in a hurry but you.

Religious doctrines. Many groups that you work with overseas will have some doctrinal differences from you. You are not there to tell them how to do church or to set them straight doctrinally. For instance, I teach my Eastern Europe teams that they should avoid talking about Bible prophecy because some Eastern European Baptists don't hold the same premillenial, pretribulational "Left Behind" doctrine that many

American evangelicals hold. We are guests here. If you don't like a picture on someone's wall when you are visiting, you don't take it down. You don't have that right. If you don't like the table setting, you don't redo it. You are a guest and have not earned the right to criticize or change.

Team-Building Preparation

If you are going to work as a team, it is important to get to know each other better and learn to work together. There is a big difference between a group and a team. A group is just an assembly of people with different goals and agendas. A team is an assembly of people who are following a common vision to complete a common goal. A team as a whole is much stronger than the sum of the individuals (study 1 Corinthians 12).

> **Keys to an Effective Team**
> 1. Common purpose
> 2. Defined roles
> 3. Purposeful leadership
> 4. Healthy relationships
> 5. Quality communication

Teams don't just happen. They are molded and formed through the purposeful plan of a good leader. Together, the people must pray, plan, train, share, worship, laugh, play, and work. This camaraderie must happen before the people ever board the airplane. Team building is one of the key purposes of the team meetings. Fun group games and informal settings like parties and retreats greatly contribute to team building.

> **Helpful Team-Building Web Resources**
> www.teamresources.com
> www.discprofile.com
> http://www.churchgrowth.org/analysis/intro.html
> www.businessballs.com/teambuildinggames.htm
> www.usscouts.org/games/game_t.html#teamg

> The most helpful team preparation/training materials are put out by:
> Culture Link
> www.culturelink.org
> (770) 973-8809

Just like a good military commander, a good leader will get to know the strength, weaknesses, and personalities of his team members; assign them appropriate tasks; and have them working together with people who complement their giftedness and personalities. Tools like the DISC Profiles test and spiritual gifts tests help the leader to understand the personality, giftedness, skills, and temperament of his team members more effectively.

CHAPTER 9

ATTITUDES, EXPECTATIONS, AND FEARS

As we go, what kind of Christianity are we exporting? Is it a faith characterized by love and the fruit of the Spirit or is it an ugly, mean-spirited, legalistic imitation of Christianity devoid of the Spirit? Jesus criticized the Jewish religious leaders.

> "You're hopeless, you religion scholars and Pharisees! Frauds! You go halfway around the world to make a convert, but once you get him you make him into a replica of yourselves, double-damned" (Matthew 23:15 *The Message*).

Please don't misunderstand Jesus. He is not condemning them for traveling over land and sea to win converts. Jesus tells His own disciples to carry the gospel to all nations and peoples. The criticism here is of zealous, yet misguided, missionaries who export just another form of religious legalism that enslaves instead of the true gospel which sets free. What kind of Christianity are we exporting?

Our witness involves far more than just the actual work we are doing—whether it be construction or handing out gospel tracts. Our witness even involves more than the message that we share verbally. Our witness is also how we act, how we treat each other, and how we respond in stress situations. Improper attitudes can ruin the witness of your team, ruin the relationships within the team, and poison the relationships with your hosts. What are our attitudes like? Do we communicate love?

Proper attitudes ultimately are a reflection of whether or not we are filled with the Holy Spirit. Team members need to ensure that they are filled with the Spirit and know how to walk in the Spirit. A person controlled by self rather than the Holy Spirit can wreck the whole project by improper attitudes. We worry about what we should bring in our flight carry-on bag. But are we concerned about what we are bringing in our spiritual carry-on bag?

> An older Chinese teacher came up, put her two hands around my face. She said, "I didn't understand everything you said. But I saw love in your eyes."

Paul writes that "the fruit of the Spirit is love, joy, peace, patience, kindness, goodness, faithfulness, gentleness and self-control" (Galatians 5:22-23). Lead your team in a group Bible discussion of Galatians 5:13–23. What do these things mean and how can we express them in our short-term mission experience?

In addition to the fruit of the Spirit as listed in Galatians, three other key attitudes especially stand out in relation to short-term mission ministry.

SERVANTHOOD

More than anything else, we must go with the attitude of a servant. If Jesus was willing to wash the feet of His disciples, we should be willing to serve one another. Go to wash feet! A superior, prima donna attitude is the kiss of death to successful short-term ministry. We must not come with the attitude, "I'm here to teach you how. We can do it better than anyone else!" Are we arriving as bulldozers, or are we coming as servant-farmers bearing precious seed. Are we going as tourists, or servants? Our attitude should be, "I'm at your disposal. We're just here to help." John 13:12-20 and Romans 2:3-11 are great passages to talk about together as a team.

Perhaps it is even better to use the word *serve* instead of the word *help*. *Serve* communicates a greater respect for the people with whom you are working. We must always avoid the attitude, "I am going to help these poor, unfortunate people."

> "The ones among you who will be really happy are those who have sought and found how to serve."—Albert Schweitzer

Servanthood means preferring others to yourself. Are you willing to allow others to go ahead of you in line, to have the better seat on the bus, to have the better sleeping arrangements, to have the better job assignment? Servanthood is putting the feelings and needs of others above your own feelings and needs.

An essential element of servanthood is humility. Do you think that because you are richer and better educated, you are better than your brother? That you deserve the better treatment? In order not to communicate a wrong idea, it is best to avoid talking about how much money you make, how many cars you may have, or how much you own. Resist showing a photo of your house. Also don't wear your best quality clothes and expensive watches or jewelry. Teams don't want to communicate a superior attitude just because God has graciously blessed them with more material things.

FLEXIBILITY

Short-term projects never go exactly the way you plan. In spite of your best planning, there are always surprises. The ministry may not go as planned. There may not be enough translators. Things are going to go wrong. After leading over 3,000 people on short-term trips, I have experienced just about everything including lost passports, illness, vehicle breakdowns, dog bites, unfriendly villagers, and even bats in hotel rooms.

The wise short-termer must not let these things get his blood pressure up. Relax. Stay calm. Perhaps *fluidity* is even a better word than *flexibility*. Go with the flow! This whole thing is in God's hands. It is His project and if He wants to allow this problem, then so be it! Sometimes God's agenda is different than ours. Expect the unexpected and you won't be caught off guard when it happens. Remember, this is a short-term adventure! Be patient. This doesn't mean that you don't address problems and try to solve them. It just means that you're not going to let it get to you. If it is out of your control, relax. If it is in the control of your hosts, point out the problem, but don't get angry with them and cause more harm by your anger than all the good that the project might accomplish. The outward expression of the inflexibility is complaining.

When my teams arrive on the field, I give them a rubber band to put on their wrists. They look a little puzzled until I explain. "When things begin to go wrong and not happen the way you expect, pull on this rubber band and let it remind you to be flexible." Some people have come back later and asked for another rubber band. They had worn out the first one.

SENSITIVITY

Be sensitive to the people with whom you are working. Get this one concept in your mind and you'll do fine: They are different—and it's OK that they are different. Different does not mean wrong or bad. It means different.

Be sensitive to their way of doing things. One short-termer observed, "When we wanted to do things differently, the missionary helped us to understand that it was the Brazilians' church, not ours." We may suggest ideas, but don't push. For instance, most Americans are very time-conscious—especially in relation to church services. Most of the rest of the world, however, is not. Learn to go at their time.

Be sensitive to their culture. Try not to purposefully offend—either in dress, language, actions, or music. Avoid criticizing. Relax. You are going to make some mistakes. As long as your attitude is right and you don't take yourself too seriously, the nationals will understand.

PRACTICAL EXPRESSIONS OF GODLY ATTITUDES

True spiritual attitudes will reflect in our actions. Here are some practical actions that are a reflection of spiritual attitudes in the context of short-term missions. These attitudes are not only critical to your witness, but also to your own spiritual focus during the project.

- I will be sensitive to theological issues. I realize that the Christian faith manifests itself in different ways in different cultures. I will avoid criticizing or debating controversial theological issues.
- I will always treat with respect my team leaders, fellow team members, in-country hosts, and nationals we work with. I will avoid criticizing my leaders, my fellow team members, and hosts.
- I will avoid any romantic activity towards fellow team members or nationals. I realize that activity of this type could hinder the team witness and interfere with my own spiritual focus on this project.
- I will not make negative political comments about my host country or excessively talk about the greatness of my

own country. I will also avoid criticizing things I do not like about my host country.

- I will never use profanity, abusive language, alcohol, tobacco products, or illegal drugs. I will also avoid watching or reading pornographic material.
- I will accept and do the jobs given to me without complaint.
- I will maintain my personal disciplines of prayer and Bible study during the project—even if it means doing it when I am tired and losing sleep.
- I will resist complaining when things go wrong or when I don't like what is happening.
- I will always obey my team leaders.
- I will always try to eat what is set before me without complaint (Luke 10:7–8).
- I will not isolate myself from nationals or missionaries during any free time, but will pursue fellowshipping with them. I won't try to spend all my time with other volunteers.

FEARS

Team members have all kinds of spoken and unspoken fears and doubts.

- How will I do? Will I be able to do good?
- I am afraid of flying.
- I am worried about the food. I require an unusual diet.
- How will my family manage with me being gone so long?
- What if an emergency comes up at home while I am gone?
- I worry about terrorists. Will I be safe? (See appendix 2.)
- I am not strong. What if I get sick?

The best solution is to get people talking about their fears instead of holding them in. Discuss with your team their fears. Also ask individual members, "How are you feeling about this? Is there anything bothering you?"

> "Anything I've ever done that ultimately was worthwhile . . . initially scared me to death."—Betty Bender

The acknowledged founder of international volunteer missions among Southern Baptists is Dub Jackson. He is a legend among those who know and study short-term missions. Jackson tells about asking an outstanding Christian farmer to join his Japan volunteer team. Jackson called the man and Woodrow agreed to go, but began to have doubts as soon as he hung up the phone. "What on earth have I done? Why have I said that I would be willing to go to Japan? I don't feel adequate in presenting the gospel here at home. What in the world could I do in Japan? Why should I go when this $1,750 could be spent better sending an outstanding preacher or musician?" Jackson writes, "He had many questions about the value of his going, but there was never a question in my mind as to his value. People like Woodrow are the heart of Partnership Evangelism. It cannot be done without them! The greatest need and the most valuable tool to be employed in winning our world to Christ is the warm-hearted, loving testimony of God's humble servants."

> "For I am the Lord, your God, who takes hold of your right hand, and says to you, Do not fear; I will help you" (Isaiah 41:13).

GREAT EXPECTATIONS

People are investing significant time and money in a short-term mission project and therefore often come with extremely high expectations. Some expect it to be a fantastic spiritual high and are disappointed when it is just plain hard work. Others may expect the people to hang on every word that drips from their lips and respond in large numbers to their message only to be surprised when little happens. Some return disappointed that they were not busier in ministry. Others return home and wonder, "How much good did I really do?"

Short-termers need to come with realistic expectations. They can be assured that they are going to work hard, it is not going to be like home, there will be some stresses, they are going to get frustrated, and things aren't going to happen as they expect.

Give your expectations to God. Trust Him to use the contribution that you make to His glory—no matter how small you think it may be. Keep Philip in mind. When God sent him into the wilderness to witness to a lone Ethiopian, it may have seemed like a waste of time and energy. But God used that one convert to bring the gospel to the continent of Africa. Philip probably never knew this. You may never know the permanent spiritual value of your short-term witness until you get to heaven.

Be prepared for disappointments. The leader may be inexperienced or incompetent, supplies may not arrive, the host may drop the ball on the ministry plan, luggage may get lost, flights may be canceled or delayed, the food and accommodations may be terrible, you might be sick, or there might be an accident. Sometimes things don't go well. Are you prepared to take the lemon and make lemonade?

Yes, go with expectations. But go with reasonable expectations. The more reasonable we are in our expectations, the fewer disappointments we will have. And most of all, allow God to work His plan and don't complain when His plan and your plan are not the same.

ATTITUDES OF THE LEADER

These same attitudes of servanthood, humility/sensitivity, and flexibility need to be held by the leader also—but in some additional ways.

Humility. The opposite of humility is prideful arrogance. Arrogance means that we think that we know all the answers and understand all of our problems and the solutions. It means that a person doesn't need advice or input because he already has it all figured out. Prideful arrogance is usually a reflection of personal insecurity and immaturity.

> "Conduct yourselves in a manner worthy of the gospel of Christ" (Philippians 1:27).

Humility, however, means that we do not have all the answers. We may not even know the right questions to ask. Humility is the attitude of a learner.

Some time ago a short-term mission director of a large church joined my trip to Eastern Europe for the first time. She came with an arrogant, inflexible attitude. "I know what I am doing. I don't want your advice. I will do things here the exact same way I do things in Central America."

Some people have ten years of experience, and others have one year of experience ten times—they never learned! It is a recipe for disaster on mission teams. It is a fatal danger when leaders live in a bubble disconnected from reality because they are not open to new information. "Don't bother me with the facts, I have my mind made up." Look out for the one-size-fits-all trap.

Are you open to evaluation and criticism? Are you willing to listen? Continuing to do your work without evaluation is like driving at night without headlights. Eventually you will crash.

Can you learn and change? Our tendency is to lead out of tradition (the way it's always been done) rather than out of vision and purpose. How do you change this? You gain new vision, purpose, and ideas through prayer, reading, dialogue with out-of-the-box thinkers, attending training conferences, and observing how others do it.

Flexibility flows out of an attitude of humility. We must adapt or die. It is true in nature—natural selection and survival of the fittest. It is true in business. It is true in missions. Can you adapt to changing situations? The person who can't be flexible

> "We naturally think we become experts by virtue of longevity. Yet a common effect of all those years of practice is an isolation and conformity to traditions." — Hans Finzel

and adapt should not serve as a team leader. Futurist Alvin Toffler says: "The illiterate of the 21st century will not be those who cannot read and write, but those who cannot learn, unlearn, and relearn."

Servanthood. Some team leaders disrespect team members and treat them as children. There was one team where the members referred to the leader privately as, " The Nazi." Drunk with power, she ran the group like the orphanage director in the movie *Annie*. Remember the words of Jesus, "Whoever wants to become great among you must be your servant" (Mark 10:43).

CHAPTER 10

LOGISTICAL ARRANGEMENTS

Who is in charge of logistical arrangements? There are two general approaches to this. Either the team leader is responsible, or you have chosen an outside organization to put things together. In Chapter 5, "Getting Started," this issue was covered in detail. Settle this issue quickly and notify the appropriate people. If the team leader is working on the logistical details, this chapter covers all the areas of responsibility. If an agent is working on the logistics, the team leader can use this chapter as a checklist.

TRAVEL DOCUMENTS: PASSPORT AND VISA

A United States passport is required in order to travel outside the United States. A passport is the proof that you are a citizen of a particular country. If you have a passport, be sure that it does not expire within six months of your travel dates. If you need a

Passport application information:
http://travel.state.gov/passport

passport, be sure to get it well before your trip departure date—several months if possible. Most passports are valid for ten years.

How do you get a passport? You must apply for a passport at a United States post office. Not all post offices, however, take passport applications. Call your local post office to find out where to go.

When you apply, you must have two passport photos, a certified copy of your birth certificate, and some other form of identification. These special-sized passport photos can be made at most camera shops, travel agencies, or photographers.

Armed with these things, go to your post office, fill out an application form, and pay your $85. You should receive a passport in the mail in several weeks. Don't forget to sign the passport in the proper place once it arrives. It is possible, in exceptional situations, to get a passport within about a week—but it will cost you!

Your passport is the most important thing you own when you travel. Lose your money before you lose your passport. Guard it with your life—well, guard it as best as you can! If you lose your passport, it is going to mean expense, great trouble, and it can disrupt the entire focus of your team. It is a good idea to keep your passport with you wherever you go. It is best to keep it in a money belt around your waist or neck.

It is also wise to make a photocopy of the cover page of your passport before you ever leave America. Store this copy somewhere in your luggage in the unhappy event that your passport is lost or stolen. It will greatly expedite replacing your passport. I also carry extra passport photos should this ever happen.

Making copies is a wise thing to do with all your important documents. What would you do if your plane ticket or wallet were stolen? Record and store in a different place your airline ticket number and also your credit card numbers. Don't forget to write down the emergency numbers on the back of your credit cards to call should they be stolen. Only carry the credit cards and calling cards that you'll need on this trip. It is also a good idea to have the phone number of the American embassy in your host country and phone numbers for your in-country hosts and hotels.

Don't let all this talk of theft scare you. I have never been ripped off personally. Travel, however, increases the possibilities of it happening. Personal violence is rare, but thieves and pickpockets are common everywhere. I want to be a good Boy Scout and be prepared should it ever happen.

A visa is permission to enter the country you are visiting. The country the team will visit issues the visa, not the US government. In many cases, you must mail your passport, visa application, photo(s), and check to that country's embassy in Washington, D.C. Some embassies are very slow processing visa applications, so get started early. Also, some countries require proof of certain immunizations before they will grant a visa.

> **Visa information:** www.embassy.org

On the visa application, you must put the purpose of visit. It is always best to put "business" or "tourist." Some countries will deny your visa application if you mention "Christian work."

AIRPLANE TICKETS

The sooner you buy airplane tickets the better. Determine when you need to buy tickets and require deposits at that time. Avoid buying tickets for team members who cannot cover the deposit. I'll talk about the cheapest way to buy tickets in the next chapter, "Airplane Tickets and Travel." The name on the ticket must match the name on the passport.

Insurance and Legal Stuff

Teams should be insured for medical emergencies, medical evacuation, and accidental death. You'll need name, birth date, and insurance beneficiary in order to get insurance. Do you need liability insurance?

Some churches want team members to sign liability release forms. For children and teenagers traveling without parents, you should get a parental medical release form that gives permission to a health-care provider to care for your child in the event of a medical emergency.

Housing Accommodations

If you are using a mission consultant, he or she will probably do all of these arrangements. But if not, then you need to work on housing, meals, and land transport. Where possible, allow your overseas hosts to make these arrangements.

If you are staying in a hotel, negotiate to get the best deal. Ask for a free room for the leader. Can you pay with credit card? Do you need to make a deposit? Always get a written room confirmation and keep it with you. Always reconfirm right before you depart the US.

If you are staying in a hotel, team members need to know several things:
- How to use the phone and costs involved.
- If they drink the water from the faucet.
- Electrical current. Often 220, and will need an adapter.
- How to keep valuables safe.
- Laundry possibilities.

Consider having your team members stay in homes of believers. I personally prefer to house people in homes if three criteria can be met.

1. Ask questions to ensure your team members will be comfort-

able in the homes. Obviously it is better not to house people in homes that are unclean, have dirt floors, no heat, poor bedding, or have mosquitoes or bugs.

2. Determine how long you will need to stay in the homes. More than four nights becomes a real burden on the hosts and is hard on the guest also. I often have my team members in the hotel the first and last nights of the project and sometimes even more if the project is long. The old proverb says that both fish and guests begin to stink after three days.

3. Consider the size of your team. The larger the group, the more difficult the logistics of finding comfortable homes and getting people around.

The advantage of staying in a home is that it creates incredible bonding with the people and begins lifelong friendships. Later many people have shared that staying with a family was the highlight of their trip. It is absolutely the best way to really get to know the people and the culture. Often short-termers are like spacemen in space suits. They remain totally insulated from the surrounding people and culture.

Staying in homes is biblical. Jesus instructed His disciples on their first short-term trip that when they came to a city they were to "search for some worthy person there and stay at his house until you leave. As you enter the home, give it your greeting. If the home is deserving, let your peace rest on it" (Matthew 10:11–13).

People often have fears about staying in a home. Will there be privacy? Can I communicate with my hosts? Will we be a burden? Yes, you may have to learn how to use an outhouse. Yes, you will be a burden, but you will be a good burden to them. And you will be a greater blessing than you are a burden. Yes, they may not speak English, but you can always find a way to communicate what you want to say—even if it is the point-and-grunt method. That is part of the fun and adventure of staying with a national host family.

Try to be a blessing to the family you stay with. Take gifts from America that they might enjoy. Gifts might include T-shirts, Christian music tapes, knives with serrated edges, ground cinnamon, can-opener, coffee, and medicine—especially acetaminophen and ibuprofen. Gifts for children might include candy, gum, balloons, toy cars, hair bows, dolls, paper dolls, T-shirts, and building blocks.

Try to leave a little cash gift to help your host family. You don't want them to be set back by buying food to take care of you. Ask your host organizer to guide you in how much money to leave. You need to realize that your host is not taking care of you for money. They are simply practicing Christian and biblical hospitality. They often will be embarrassed and refuse the money. Just leave it in a prominent place where it can be found after you have left.

MEALS

What is the plan for feeding your group? Are they eating in homes? Restaurants? Churches? Preparing their own meals? A few people are easy to feed but a group requires a lot of planning.

My groups have called me "McKirby" because I use a certain fast-food restaurant so much with my teams as we are traveling. When you are traveling overseas with a large group of people, this restaurant provides three essential things: fast service, clean rest rooms, and safe, familiar food.

LAND TRANSPORTATION

How will your group get around? How will they get to the airport from your home? How will they get from the overseas airport to their ministry location? Is there adequate room for luggage? How will they get around each day? Do you need to rent a bus? Vans? Taxis? How much will it cost? How much do you reimburse people for using their private cars? Will the missionary host use his own vehicle to help your team? Disorganized land transportation can really upset a group.

Ministry Arrangements

Who is setting up the ministry plan? How detailed a ministry schedule do you have? Is it a realistic plan? Does it involve all your team and use their giftedness most effectively? Is there a lot of dead time where they have nothing to do? Are some working and others just standing around with their hands in their pockets? What does a typical daily work schedule look like?

Do you need interpreters, and who is organizing this? What is the quality of the interpreters? What are your expectations of them? What financial arrangements need to be made with them?

Who is communicating with the national leaders with whom you will work?

What supplies/tools do you need to do your intended work? Who is getting them? Realize that construction projects create a whole new list of arrangement requirements.

Communications

Do you have all the phone numbers that you need? Proper dialing codes? Do the families back home have emergency numbers where team members may be reached?

Just Call

Any time you feel nervous about how things are coming

together, pick up the phone and call. If you are not getting the information you need, pick up the phone and call. A short international phone call is a small price to pay for your peace of mind that things are being planned appropriately. A phone call also reminds your helper overseas not to procrastinate.

COMMISSIONING SERVICE ARRANGEMENTS

In Acts 13, the church leaders laid hands on and prayed for those who were about to leave to carry the gospel far, far away. "They placed their hands on them and sent them off" (Acts 13:3). It means a great deal to a deal to have one's home church formally commission a team. Commissioning is a formal endorsement of the team by the home church.

A commissioning might include an introduction of the project and of the team members, Scripture reading, a short exhortation to the team, a reminder to the church to pray for the team, and then a prayer led by the pastor. Church leaders might gather around the team and lay hands on them as the pastor prays.

PARTING WORDS

Here are a few administrative principles: Plan your work and then work your plan. Success and failure are in the details. Procrastination will get you in trouble. Never assume that your requests will be done the first time. Confirm and reconfirm arrangements. Always be thinking through a plan B in case something goes wrong. Only exhibit visible anger when it will solve a problem, not make it worse.

Have a good trip and go with God.

CHAPTER 11

AIRPLANE TICKETS AND TRAVEL

This chapter covers two major topics. First, we'll cover how to get the best deals on plane tickets for your group. Second, we'll discuss helpful information on international air travel to make your long journey more pleasant.

WHERE TO BUY TICKETS

The answer to that depends upon how many people you have going and how complicated a flight program you have. If you have a small group, are experienced with the destination, can use the same airline, and are going to a major city destination such as Mexico City, Amsterdam, etc., then you may find the best deal buying tickets online. You may choose to buy direct from the airline Web page or from one of the large online travel agencies.

Online Travel Reservations
www.expedia.com
www.orbitz.com
www.travelocity.com
www.kls2.com/airlines/

However, for most trips, you need to use a mission specialist or a travel agent. There is a "missionary fare" that travel agents can get that often is the best deal during the summer months. Understand, however, that not all travel agents are experienced in mission travel or in your particular destination. It usually ends up costing more money using a local travel agent out of your church instead of an agency that does a large bulk of international travel and is able to get good discounts and concessions from the airlines. Also, even if you use a travel agent, you need to do your own online research and know what the rock-bottom prices are—so that you can help keep your travel agent from making any mistakes that might cost you money.

Mission Travel Agencies

Intermissions: intermissions worldtravel.com

MTS Travel: www.mtstravel.com

Raptim Travel: www.raptimusa.com

Fellowship Travel: www.fellowship.com

AIRLINE CHOICES

Sometimes, cheapest is not best. You may save $50 on the ticket, but lose a day or find yourself stranded overseas. What is the reputation of the airline? For instance, Air Zimbabwe has the cheapest fares to Zimbabwe. However, the president of the country has a habit of commandeering the plane whenever he wants to go somewhere—stranding ticketed passengers. Lesson: Third-World airlines should be avoided whenever possible.

I remember a time several years ago when Air France lost bags on eight consecutive teams that I was leading. I used to joke that we were flying Air Chance, Flight 5050—because we had a 50-50 chance of the bags arriving. I must say that Air France has greatly improved since that time.

When to Buy

There are two ways to approach buying airplane tickets:

1. Estimate your group size, and put a deposit down well in advance with the travel agent or airline to hold seats at an agreed-upon price. This is the best way to do things if you are traveling to a popular destination during a high travel time—such as summer. Usually, the balance for the plane ticket is not due until a month before departure.

2. Buy the tickets on a sale. To do this, you need names (as they appear on the passport) and full payment. The problem here is that you gamble that they will have seats available, and seats at a better price. This is the cheapest way to buy tickets, but never do it in summer. The best time to get deals is in the off-season when airlines are trying to fill up empty seats. There are almost no deals in the summer.

How to Get Airfare Deals

Your plane ticket will be the single most expensive part of your short-term mission adventure. If you can be flexible and aggressive, you can find deals. Timing is everything when it comes to getting the best deals on tickets. Here are several hints that may help you keep the cost down.

1. If possible, plan your project during the season when airfares are lowest to your destination. For instance, in Europe this is between November 1 and March 15. Airfares to Europe are more expensive in the summer—sometimes triple as much as the off-season fares. Also the planes are not nearly as full in the off-season and seats for groups are much easier to find. Students should consider spring-break projects instead of summer projects if possible.

   Winter is really a good time for mission projects in Central and Eastern Europe. The winter causes people to be at home and to have time to attend church services and to talk about spiritual things. According to a Romanian proverb, "Winter is the springtime of the soul."

2. You can get better deals if you have flexibility on your travel dates. Most airlines have a tiered system of pricing. The cheapest seats are sold first, then prices go up as demand for seats goes up. Also seats are more difficult to get and prices are usually higher on Friday through Monday. Seats are easier to get and cheaper on Tuesday through Thursday.

3. Watch for sales and then act immediately. You can sign up with the FareWatcher program in travelocity.com to be alerted online to sales to your chosen destinations. Newspapers also usually advertise sales—especially *USA Today*. It is a rare travel agent who calls you when a sale begins. You must be alert to a sale.

   If you require team members to pay their airline money early, this gives you the flexibility to buy the tickets when they go on sale. When a sale comes, seats go quickly, so you must act promptly to buy the ticket. The larger the group, the harder it is to take advantage of sales—because seats usually are limited and go quickly. If you don't already have money from team members, get on the phone immediately when you discover a sale and tell the team members that you can cut the project cost if they can get you ticket money ASAP.

4. Most economy-priced or sale-priced tickets are nonchangeable and also nonrefundable. Changes on the return can often be done for an extra charge. Never buy tickets for your team members until you have their money in hand (at least for the airfare), or unless your church is willing to absorb the cost if the person backs out.

5. Some airlines give 1 free ticket for 20 (or 25) paid tickets—although I am finding that this practice is declining (this also often works with hotel rooms). Ask your travel agent to

negotiate this for you. Don't expect any success, however, if you are getting an off-season rock-bottom sale price.

6. Buy your tickets on a credit card. This gives you some protection if anything goes wrong and often provides flight insurance. Best of all, most airlines now have deals with credit card companies that allow frequent flyer mileage credit for dollars charged. The Delta SkyMiles Credit Card (from American Express), for example, gives two frequent flyer miles for every dollar charged buying a Delta ticket. United and Northwest have Visa affinity cards. If your group is large enough, you can earn a free ticket by just paying for the group on an affinity credit card. Most airline Web sites have information about their affinity credit cards.

SEAT SELECTION

When you have to sit in the same seat for hours at a time, seat selection becomes important. Request your seat location when you book your flight. Aisle or window seats are the most popular. Avoid the dreaded middle seats.

If you are traveling alone and want a possible empty seat next to you, then request center section, aisle, towards the back of the airplane. The center aisle seats towards the back will be the last seats assigned by the airline and may be empty if the flight is not full.

FREQUENT FLYER

On their second trip, people tell, "I wish I had signed up for the frequent flyer program on the first trip! I'd have a free ticket now." I am a great fan of frequent flyer programs. Two trips to Europe may earn you a free domestic ticket. Also, get an affinity credit card and gain miles as you spend. Most affinity credit cards

Some Affinity Credit Cards
Delta SkyMiles Credit Card
from American Express
United Mileage Plus Visa
Northwest World Perks Visa
Diner's Club Card

will give you 10,000 to 15,000 points just for taking out the card.

You must sign up for the program and get a number before you travel. You can easily sign up for the airline's frequent flyer program at the airline Web site. Give this number each time you check in. Also, keep your passenger coupon and boarding passes as proof if your miles fail to show up in your account.

BAGGAGE CHECK-IN

Generally, you are allowed two checked bags and one carry-on bag. You may also carry a camera case, briefcase, purse, or some other small bag. Fifty pounds is the maximum permitted weight per bag on domestic flights. Most airlines permit 70 pounds per bag on international flights and domestic flights that are connecting to international flights. Recently some airlines have lowered the international weight allowance to 50 pounds per bag. Many non-USA airlines limit you to 44 pounds total baggage and charge substantially for excess baggage unless you are part of an ongoing, unbroken international flight. Check with each of your scheduled airlines on their baggage policies.

Web Air Travel Advice
www.howtoadvice.com/AirTravel
www.independenttraveler.com/resources

Your carry-on bag needs to be sized so that it can fit under the seat if necessary. If you push the size envelope on this, be prepared to possibly have the bag taken away at the gate as checked baggage. Some foreign airlines are also particular about carry-on baggage weight. Try to be one of the first to board a long international flight because storage space in the overhead bins fills up very quickly and it gets rather uncomfortable having a bag under your feet for eight hours.

If your team needs to take more than two bags per person,

then you should make arrangements with the airline in advance. It is best to do this when you are negotiating the ticket. Sometimes airlines will allow mission groups free bags; but if not, be prepared to pay about $100 per bag.

It is wise not to take more luggage than you can carry by yourself. Don't count on help with your bags. Bags with wheels are essential.

When you are checking in as part of a team, it is always helpful to appoint a luggage captain. He has the following responsibilities in order to ensure that no bags are lost:

- Make sure each piece of team luggage (including carry-ons) has a name tag and also a piece of bright surveyor's flagging marking it.
- Counts how many pieces of luggage the team has and sees that the luggage is moved from point A to point B. This involves counting bags every time the team moves.
- Is responsible for baggage security.
- Oversees loading and unloading of bags.

Packing Advice

I usually start a packing list several weeks before departure. I write down things that I need as they come to mind. I also set up a special box or a piece of luggage for trip items. Some important things that are often forgotten include earplugs, family photos, alarm clock, sunscreen, mosquito spray, extra film, flashlight, hand wipes, roll of toilet paper (you never know when it will come in handy), and a washcloth. Many foreign hotels do not provide washcloths. Appendix 15 is a sample packing list.

Don't forget to research the weather forecast in the cities you are visiting. This information can easily found on the Internet (www.wunderground.com). Always remember to take enough clothes to keep warm. You can take it off if you have it, but you can't put it on if you don't have it. Long underwear has saved my life on more than one occasion.

I tell my teams to put their personal stuff in one checked bag. The other checked bag is reserved for ministry supplies and team purposes. There is no reason ever to need more than one suitcase for personal items or clothes. An important piece of advice is to pack as light as you can. Ask yourself the question, "Can I live without this?" You don't need as much as you think you need. A good rule is to pack only for one week. You can reuse and wash clothes. Pack liquid and powder items in plastic bags. Inventory and mark ministry bags before you leave home so that you do not have to open all the bags to find certain items.

> "If you are going to a country where Christianity is not welcomed, divide religious materials among personal luggage. This way it won't appear like a religious library is moving in."—Larry Ragan

Be sure to label your bags with your home address and your destination address. Mark team bags with a strip of orange surveyor's flagging. Security these days requires that the bags be unlocked. Never put anything of serious value in your checked bags—especially if you are traveling to or from a Third-World country. Hopefully, the second bag used for group ministry supplies will come home empty. Therefore consider bringing bags that you can put inside of each other on the return flight. Also, if possible, use normal suitcases. Boxes and plastic cartons are red flags to customs agents.

Packing your carry-on bag requires special care. Don't forget the size requirement. Also, remember that this bag will receive special security scrutiny. Nothing that could be used as a weapon or even resemble a weapon can go in this bag (i.e., scissors, pocketknife, etc.). In case your checked bag is lost (which is rare, but possible), carry absolutely indispensable items in your carry-on (i.e., toiletries, teaching notes, important papers, Bible, contact lens supplies, change of underwear, medicines, all small valuables, fragile items, travel documents, passport). It is also good to carry a light jacket or sweater on the plane—even in summer. Don't forget something to entertain you for the long flight—such as books, crossword puzzle book, magazines, and iPod. Camera and all film should go in the carry-on bag, never in your checked bag.

AIRPORT SECURITY

If you have not flown recently, things are much different today due to September 11. Airport security can be time-consuming and stressful if you are not prepared beforehand. On a departing international flight from a major airport, you should arrive at the airport 3 hours early—especially if you are traveling at a busy time. Arriving early reduces stress dramatically and helps you to be more patient when things go wrong. Prepare your team for the security checks they'll face at the airport and remind them to just relax and let the security people do their job. When they search you and/or your bags, it is not personal. They are just doing their job. It goes smoother if you empty your pockets into your carry-on bag and go through the security checkpoint just holding your ticket and passport. Never make wisecracks about terrorists, hijacking, Cuba, bombs, or weapons.

Never leave your bags unattended. If you must bunch your bags at an airport or hotel, put them all against a wall and appoint someone to watch.

GOLDEN RULE TRAVEL ETIQUETTE

You are going to spend a lot of hours squeezed next to other people on the airplane. Here are a few people I hope you do not meet.

- Territorial Tom. When the guy took the seat next to me he really took it. He took it all . . . and then some. I never saw the armrest again on the flight. I am not territorial about armrests. I am willing to share. I'm even willing leave it vacant as body space buffer. But not Tom.

- Rocking Robin. As soon as the plane lifted off, he pushed the seat back all the way into my face and knees. It stayed that way the next eight hours—even during meals. The man was big and nervous, and the seat was loose. So, he rocked in the seat the entire trip. Each rock brought him another three inches closer to me.
- Beanie Bob. My mom always taught me to wear clean underwear and not eat beans before I fly. I don't even want to think about the purpose of the clean underwear.
- Smelly Susan. Honey, please take a shower before you fly. I've got to endure eight hours of BO.
- Chatty Kathy. Dear Chatty: If your seatmate looks uninterested, please stop talking to him. He may want to read or rest. Also, if he dims the lights, it means he wants to sleep.

So what do these fellow travelers teach us? You are going to be squeezed together for a long, long time. Be thoughtful of the people around you. Treat them as you would like them to treat you.

FLIGHT SAFETY AND COMFORT

Never accept bags or packages from strangers to take on the plane. Once seated, listen to the safety speech. Also, before takeoff, try to locate the nearest emergency exit and think through a personal evacuation plan were something to happen. Having said that, realize that statistically you would have to take a passenger jet flight every day for 26,000 years before you would crash.

Wear comfortable clothes and shoes for the trip. Bring plenty of things to keep you entertained. Always leave your seat belt on when not moving around. On the other hand, don't hesitate to get up and walk around or stand in commons area on the plane. This is especially important if you have circulatory problems.

Try to sleep on overnight flights if possible. Earplugs, eye covers, and sleeping pills will help. Sometimes it is easier to sleep at a window seat.

JET LAG

Welcome to the wonderful reality of international travel! Jet lag is the delightful experience that occurs when you travel east or across multiple time zones and confuse the body's inner time clock. For instance, when it is 6:00 P.M. in Atlanta, it is 1:00 A.M. in Athens. When you go quickly from here to there, your body struggles to make the adjustment. Traveling north and south without crossing time zones does not create jet lag.

Jet lag means your body arrives in worse shape than your luggage. Jet lag will make you feel like your body is here in America, your mind overseas, and your stomach somewhere in between. You feel bad, irritable, and tired. You forget things. It can disturb your appetite. When you come home, you want to sleep when everybody else is awake. You wake up while everyone else is sleeping. Your body is out of whack.

> "Jet lag is nature's way of making you look like your passport photo."—Linda Perret

If I knew a secret to overcoming jet lag, I would write a book and be a rich man. Unfortunately, there are no easy ways to beat jet lag. Reconcile yourself to the fact that you are going to be very tired and have sleep problems the first few days after your international journey. If possible, avoid returning to work the day after arriving home. If you are a doctor, I sure wouldn't want you doing surgery on me the afternoon after arriving home!

There are some things, however, that will help. Begin your journey well-rested. Try to sleep on the plane if it is night outside. Avoid alcohol and caffeine on the plane. Drink lots of water, and eat light. Get up and walk around and exercise on the flight. Once you arrive, force yourself to adjust to the time schedule where you now are. Change your watch and alarm clock to the local time. Avoid naps during the day. If you must nap, take a short catnap. Exercise and sunlight really help. If necessary, use sleeping pills or melatonin to help your body adjust to the new time. It is a problem when it is midnight on the field, you can't sleep, you have a busy day tomorrow, and yet, on your body clock it is only 5:00 P.M.

PASSPORT CONTROL AND CUSTOMS

One of the reasons why America is such a wonderful place is because we can easily travel around our vast country without ever crossing an international border. We can go from state to state freely.

When you enter another country, however, that country has the right to screen you before they let you in their country. They will require that you produce a passport which proves who you are and identifies what nationality you are. Some foreign countries also require that Americans get visas in order to visit their country. A visa is a document issued by that country's embassy which gives you permission to enter their country. Not all countries, however, require a visa. For instance, Russia requires a visa but Romania does not. Some countries also require a letter of invitation from a recognized host agency within the country. Your visa application should indicate that the purpose of your trip is "tourist" or "visit." Do not indicate that you are going as a missionary or doing religious work as this could delay your application or prejudice the consul's decision on granting your visa.

When you arrive in a foreign country by air, the first place you will go upon disembarking the plane will be passport control.

Here they will check your passport and visa (if required). This is not the time or place for jokes. Stay quiet unless you are asked a question. You then proceed to the baggage area where you will reclaim your bags. Don't leave the baggage area until you can account for all your bags. If you have a missing bag, go to the lost baggage desk and make a claim. Ask them to deliver the lost bag to your in-country address. Be sure to have that address with you.

Then, with your bags, you will go through customs. Customs is concerned with what you are bringing into or out of the country. If asked, tell them that they are just personal belongings. Customs has the right to search your bags. In the old days of Communism, religious literature and Bibles found in your bags could cause you to be put on the next plane home. If they ask you about money, just show them your credit card and say nothing else unless asked. Don't volunteer information, but be truthful when asked direct questions. Your group needs to go through customs together. When the group has all its bags, then lead the group to customs as a train. Tell the official that you are a group. Ninety-five percent of the time they wave us through as a group without looking at a bag.

Items of value, such as laptop computers, video cameras, and large amounts of money must be declared to customs, if you intend to bring these things back out when you leave. You will receive papers which will help you to bring your possessions back out of the country without exceptional hassle.

You will go through this procedure again when you leave the country. They will be concerned that you have been in their country legally, and that you are not taking out of their country things of significant value that you acquired there—without first paying taxes on what you acquired.

You will also go through passport control and customs as you reenter the United States. You will probably be given a customs declaration on the airplane. You will be required to declare and pay taxes on all that you have acquired on your trip worth over $1,000. They will also be concerned that you are not bringing in any food items and agricultural products that could harbor disease or insects. For more information, go to www.cbp.gov/xp/cgov/travel.

CHAPTER 12

HEALTH AND SAFETY

In this chapter we will talk about two things: how to stay healthy and how to stay safe.

If you get sick, you will not enjoy the project. You will waste precious time being sick, and you will not accomplish what you came for. I've had team members spend the whole trip in bed sick, and it was really, really frustrating to them.

You are more susceptible to getting sick on a short-term mission trip. The stress, exhaustion, and exposure to new germs make you a prime target. You may be exposed to health risks in developing areas of the world where levels of sanitation and services are lower and food and water controls may be absent. Reprogram yourself to be aware of the dangers.

As team leader, you need a healthy team in order to accomplish your mission. Take care of the mules that pull the plow. Here is some advice for caring for the mules.

Travel Health Information
www.cdc.gov/travel
www.who.int/ith
http://healthlink.mcw.edu/
www.travelmedicine.com

Vaccinations and Medicines

There are some nasty diseases lurking in some Third-World places. Find out from online sources and from your overseas host what shots are needed. Remember, however, that these sources are like doctors. In order to protect themselves from liability, they will tell you every possible thing you can get in that country—however unlikely the chances.

How do you know what shots you should get? You are low risk if you are staying a short time, living in a clean healthy environment, and your work will be in a relatively clean place with minimal physical contact with very poor or sick people. You are at higher risk if you stay a longer period of time and/or work close with sick people or work in unsanitary environments. Medical teams certainly should protect themselves. Always follow the health advice of your missionary host.

What are some shots you might need? Everyone should have had a tetanus shot in the past ten years. Most people going to Third-World countries will need some medicine for malaria. Other shots needed might include cholera, typhoid, hepatitis A, and yellow fever. You can usually get the necessary shots from your personal physician or (more cheaply) from your county health department.

If vaccinations are required, then it is important to get an International Certificate of Vaccination from your health department or travel agent. Your vaccinations should be registered in this document. Keep this document with you.

Begin Fresh and Healthy

It is best to depart on a missions trip in good health. Take vitamin C and multipurpose vitamins for several days before leaving. Also encourage people to walk and exercise in order to get in shape. A good night's sleep before you fly is the best thing you can do to stay healthy and also to minimize jet lag. This means don't save packing until the last minute!

Healthy Flying

Many short-termers begin getting sick on the flight to their destination. They start the trip stressed and exhausted, don't sleep on the plane, and are exposed to all sorts of germs in a very confined area. By the time they arrive at their destination, they are dehydrated, exhausted, and sick with a cold or something worse. Much of this can be prevented.

Stress is a huge factor in making us susceptible to illness. Reduce stress by beginning the trip fresh, rested, and reducing rush that creates stress. Get to the airport early. Try to sleep on the plane. Drink lots of water—beginning a day before the flight. Wash you hands often, especially after the toilet. Getting up and walking around hourly helps to prevent possible blood clots. If you are seated next to someone who is obviously sick, ask to be moved.

If you have ear or sinus problems, see your doctor before your trip. Aircraft pressure changes can be quite painful. If you have a cold, take a decongestant before you fly. Yawning can help to equalize the pressure in your ears when you descend.

Water

Unless you are in the United States, Canada, Japan, or Western Europe, only drink bottled water. Be alert that some homes and restaurants you visit serve tap water in bottled water containers—thus fooling you that the water is good. If you don't break the seal yourself, consider the water unsafe. Many nationals don't understand the problems we have with their water. It doesn't trouble them. Why should it trouble us? Bottled water with gas (carbonation) is very common overseas. If you don't like it, ask for water with no gas.

I encourage team members to carry a small bottle of water on the plane. Keep it and refill it during the trip from large water bottles. Team leader, be sure that your overseas host has bottled water for everyone as soon as they exit the airport. My experience is that people get off the airplane dehydrated and very thirsty.

Avoid using ice cubes. Use bottled water to brush you teeth. I had one team member use precious bottled drinking water to wash her hair. You don't have to go that far!

Tap water is OK if it is boiled or treated with chemicals such as halazone or tetraglycine hydroperiodide. Otherwise, do not drink. Hot tea and coffee are OK. Also, bottled drinks and carbonated soft drinks are fine.

Foods

One of the most common questions that prospective short-termers ask concerns food. Will I be able to eat the food? I tell my teams going to Eastern Europe that they will gain weight instead of lose weight. This is not always the case, but I think most people are pleasantly surprised to discover that their fears about food are mostly groundless.

Every short-termer has his food stories. I've been fed pig brains in Eastern Europe and been served tea with floating flies in an African mud hut. I've been served goat meat that smelled horrible and I've eaten mapone worms (actually caterpillars). These culinary blessings are rare, however. Usually the food is familiar and OK. If you are staying in a hotel, you have some control over the menu. If you are visiting a home, be assured that you are honored guests and the people will give you their very best. They may even blow their monthly food budget and do without for several weeks in order to serve you the best. Your responsibility is not to offend them and do your best to eat it (Luke 10:7–8).

The general principle is to avoid offending your hosts if at all possible. One short-termer put it this way. "Where He leads, I will follow. What they feed, I will swallow!" Sometimes you just have to eat something that isn't too attractive. There are other times, however, when you just have to say no (upset stomach is a good reason). There are other times when you can dodge the bullet if you are wise. The tea with the flies discreetly got dumped out the door when my host wasn't looking. The foul-smelling goat meat discreetly was fed to a passing dog. The pig brains, however, had to be eaten. Surprise! Surprise! It wasn't really that bad—except for the mushy texture! The mapone caterpillars were crunchy.

I have found some general principles have held me in good stead in my many travels. Most of these lessons have been learned the hard way. For instance, always insist on small portions. If you like it, you can get more. But if it is bad, you're in big trouble. When the food does taste good, don't eat large amounts. You may pay for it later. Moderation in all things (including eating) is a wonderful virtue for short-termers. If it smells bad, don't eat it. Avoid eating fatty sausage and fish or drinking milk or milk products. Avoid salads and be selective about other fresh fruits and vegetables, eating only those that can be peeled or are cooked. Avoid out-of-the-way eating places, food buffets, and street vendors of food. Avoid foods that spoil easily. Avoid foods that are not thoroughly cooked and piping hot. If in doubt, ask your missionary host. Do not ask a national.

COLDS

Colds are very common on mission trips. A cold will really take the fun out of a mission trip, so it is worth taking precautions. Here are some things that I've learned that have helped me to stay healthier.

- Begin the trip rested and try to get adequate rest during the project. This helps to strengthen the body's resistance to colds.
- Use preventative supplements such as vitamin C, echinacea, and zinc.
- Avoid close contact with people who have colds. Stay as far away from coughers and sneezers as you can. People are more contagious the first few days of a cold.
- Wash hands often—even obsessively. Always have hand wipes and antibacterial hand sanitizer with you.
- Avoid touching your eyes/mouth/nose with your hands. Germs are transferred this way. If you must touch your face, use your knuckle! If you want to catch a cold, shake hands with everybody after the church service and then rub your eyes with your hands.
- Beware of dishcloths and hand towels. They are teeming with cold germs! Perhaps carry your own hand towel.
- Use zinc tablets at the first symptom of a cold. There is good evidence that this can stave off or shorten the length of the cold. Continue to take it every few hours. First symptoms may include chilling, flushed feeling, sneezing, cold extremities—such as your hands and nose—and achiness.
- The low humidity of airplanes dries out your nasal passages and creates a fertile place for cold germs to grow. Mist your nostrils with saline nasal spray frequently during the flight. Drink lots of water.
- Exercise. Researchers at the University of South Carolina found a test group that got moderate exercise averaged one cold a year, while those less active reported four colds.

Diarrhea and Food Poisoning

The Centers for Disease Control (CDC) estimates that up to 50 percent of international travelers develop diarrhea—usually in the first week of their travel. Ninety percent of travelers' diarrhea stems from contaminated food or water. The odds are very good that you are going to have some kind of problem.

The best prevention advice for both diarrhea and food poisoning is to obey the food and water advice previously mentioned. Make wise food and drink choices. If you have a problem, first try over-the-counter loperamide (Imodium). If that does not work, then use a prescription drug such as diphenoxylate hydrochloride and atropine (Lomotil). Be very alert to the possibility of dehydration. For more information, see www.cdc.gov/travel/foodwater.htm.

Nausea

Motion sickness is common with team members. If someone is prone to motion sickness, encourage them to use dimenhydrinate (Dramamine). If the group has a long bus or van drive, encourage the person to sit at the front. Also keep a barf bag with travel stuff—just in case. It is also good idea to keep a prescription antinausea medicine in your team medical kit.

Malaria

Malaria is a very serious problem in many places of the world. According to the CDC, "Malaria is a major international public health problem." The female Anopheles mosquito transmits the malaria disease (the female has no buzz, so it is the one you don't hear that gets you!). If you are bitten by a carrier mosquito, the first malaria attack may feel like a bad case of the flu. It may include shaking chills, high fever, fatigue, headache, muscle ache, gastrointestinal symptoms, and dry cough. Untreated, you will have reoccurring cycles of attacks every few days, weeks, or months.

You don't need to be afraid of malaria, but you do need to take precautions to protect yourself. Two words should come to mind as you deal with avoiding malaria: *prevention* and *protection*. The best prevention, obviously, is to avoid being bitten. An ounce of prevention is worth a pound of cure. Most bites occur at night while you are sleeping. If you are in a malaria-prone area, use mosquito repellent with DEET on exposed skin at all times. After dark, be sure that exposed skin on arms, legs, etc., is covered. Any sweet smelling substance you use on your body attracts mosquitoes. Don't open widows at night unless you have screens. For sure, don't turn on the light in your room unless you have the windows shut or screens (without any holes) on the windows. Visually check your room for mosquitoes. Spray your room and use slow burning mosquito coils. A mosquito net over your bed is both romantic and functional.

Not only should you take steps to prevent being bitten, but you also should take drugs that will help protect you if you are bitten. Several malaria prophylaxis (prevention) drugs are available: Chloroquine, Lariam, Mefloquine, Doxycycline, Malarone, etc. These do not prevent the contracting of malaria, but they do prevent the majority of patients from becoming ill until the parasite has gone through its cycle and is eliminated from the body. Each drug has a different set of instructions and also possible side effects. Aside from Doxycycline, these drugs are not cheap if bought in the United States. The Centers for Disease Control (CDC) Web site on malaria is outstanding: www.cdc.gov/malaria/facts.htm.

Dehydration/Sunburn

Many of the climates that teams work in are hot and sunny. The sun in the tropics and at high altitudes can be vicious. Often the work is outdoors and team members are doing work that is more physical and not normal for them. I've had team members with serious sunburn, dehydration, and at the emergency room with heat stroke. If you are using Doxycycline as your malaria prophylaxis, it may make you more sensitive to the sun.

Most advice is common sense. Wear sunscreen and a hat when working outdoors and stay hydrated. If your urine is yellowish, then you are not drinking enough fluids. Always have a water of bottle with you. Listen to your body and don't try to be a hero if you are feeling bad. Get in the shade, take a break, and drink, drink, drink. Are sunglasses offensive in the culture you are working in?

I had some women on one team in Africa who told me that they held it all day and never went because the toilets were so smelly and bad. That is a bad idea that can set you up for some serious urinary tract infections.

AIDS

AIDS is a giant problem in some places—especially Africa. Some countries have 30 to 50 percent of the population with AIDS. One preacher told me he would never go to Africa because of AIDS. I thought about Jesus touching the lepers and how fear should never stop us from helping the most needy and rejected. They need our message more than any others! I remember doing street evangelism in Africa and visiting with a man who had AIDS. We shared the gospel, led him to Christ, and left a Bible and sweatshirt. Three days later our missionary host went back to visit the man and found that he had died.

The reality, however, is that AIDS is absolutely no danger to us unless we are having intercourse with the locals or are exposed to blood. If we are around people who are bleeding, or if we have an accident and we are bleeding, then we should be very, very careful. Never touch another person's blood unless you are protected. A good thing is to keep a pair of medical rubber gloves with you at all times.

In the event of needing a blood transfusion, consider having team members donate blood instead of using unknown blood. Medical evacuation is better than a blood transfusion.

Of course dental and medical teams who are exposed to blood in their ministry should take special precautions. Check out the CDC Web site for information.

MEDICAL EMERGENCY PLAN

Team members should have personal medical kits, but also all teams should have a team medical kit and a team member appointed keep the kit and help treat team members. I'm always thrilled when I have a medical doctor on a team, but sometimes I am happy to settle for a wise, experienced mother. See appendix 16 for a suggested list of items for your team medical kit.

On their application forms, team members should tell you their blood type and any other major medical problems that they have. What information do you need to know to have them treated away from home—especially if they are incapacitated? If you are taking minors, you should have a medical treatment release form signed by their parents. As leader, be sure to keep with you the team insurance information and emergency contact numbers. It is good to have extra money with you to pay emergency medical bills. Even if you have team medical insurance, the hospital/health provider will probably want some payment at the time of treatment. Does your team insurance cover emergency medical evacuation? Talk with your overseas host beforehand and agree on a plan for handling medical emergencies. Can your team members reach you in the event of a injury or an emergency?

We have looked at how to travel healthy. Now let's look at how to travel safely.

VEHICULAR TRAVEL

The most dangerous thing you do on the mission field will be traveling in automobiles. Automobile accidents are the leading cause of death among missionaries. Except in very unusual situations, avoid driving yourself. Allow others to drive you. It is safer to use hired, professional drivers. Insist on safe, quality vehicles for your team. When riding in cars, always use your seat belt and choose the backseat when you can.

If using a hired driver, always tell him before beginning the journey, "The Americans are not used to the way of driving here and they will not enjoy the journey if you go too fast. Please drive slower and more careful than normal."

Teach your teams to do everything possible to avoid offending your national hosts, but break that rule when it comes to automobile safety. Team leader, you must speak if the driver is irresponsible and/or unsafe. I had a hired van driver once that would not listen to my complaints to slow down and drive more carefully. Finally I told him, "If I speak one more time about your driving, I will not pay the bill." He slowed down!

WALKING

My pastor friend and his wife had just arrived in London. They were crossing a busy street and by habit looked left. They never saw the car that hit them. They forgot that in England, people drive on the other side. Fortunately, they woke up in the hospital with only serious bruises.

Please, be very careful walking in other countries. In most places, pedestrians do not have the right of way. Even at marked crosswalks, do not assume that the drivers will stop. Always obey crosswalks and crossing signals. Team members are fascinated and dazed by their new surroundings, entranced with the sights, and often are not paying attention when they are walking. When leading groups walking through cities, often they do not keep up and string out behind the leader. It is a recipe for disaster!

Be alert to the danger of an ankle or leg injury walking—especially at night in unlighted areas. Remember your mother's advice, "Watch where you are going." One missionary told how she broke her leg stepping into an uncovered manhole walking at night. Always carry a flashlight at night. Also, good sturdy walking shoes may protect you from an injury.

PERSONAL SECURITY

I became a security nagger after leading my very first international team. One man had his suitcase stolen off the trailer while we were parked at a border crossing. A woman had her purse stolen in an Amsterdam hotel lobby. I actually watched the theft afterwards on the hotel security camera. Her tickets and passport were in the stolen purse. Big problem!

Since then, I have been somewhat paranoid and nag my teams relentlessly about security issues. But I've led over a hundred teams since then and have had very few problems. Here are the things that I tell my team members:

- Don't walk alone.
- Avoid walking in "bad" areas. Listen to your instincts. If you find yourself in a situation that makes you feel uneasy, get out quick and don't talk as you depart.
- Avoid walking at night in cities—except in groups and in well-lighted public areas.

- Always use a money belt.
- Never flash your money in public places. When you pay for something, always hold your money near your body. Pulling a large wad of money out of your money belt on a busy street sidewalk instantly makes you a target!
- Never change money on the street or in a public place.
- Avoid leaving valuables in your hotel room. Use the hotel safe. If you do leave valuables in your room, they should be zipped away in your bag, not in plain sight.
- Never put your bags or purse out of your sight. Purses are special targets especially in hotel lobbies and on public transportation. Even at church, don't forget about watching and praying.
- Briefcases and laptop computers seem to be especially tempting targets. Especially watch your briefcase at train stations and your laptop at airport security screening areas.
- Be alert to people "crowding" you in public places or on public transportation. Thieves often do this to pick your pocket or to slash your fanny pack or wallet pocket with a razor blade to empty it. Babies are often used by pickpockets to distract.
- Be wary of strangers who offer to help you. A stranger offered to help me as I was trying to use a machine to buy commuter train tickets in Vienna, Austria, with my credit card. A month later I had over $10,000 worth of charges on my card in Spain. I have never been to Spain in my life!
- Never go alone with strangers to dark or secluded places. I know of one short-term missionary who was seriously mugged and beat up when he broke this rule.
- Don't dress or carry baggage that makes you look rich. Dress down and use older, worn bags.
- Try not to advertise yourself as a "tourist." This is especially important in crowded public places and on public

transportation. Thieves in the area will immediately see you as a target. A camera hanging around your neck is a dead giveaway. Also, most Americans are loud and boisterous. Try to avoid talking loudly in English in public places. It can make you a target. Incidentally, loud talking is associated with drunkenness in many cultures.

- Loading and unloading at airports, train stations, and hotels are high theft danger times. Keep your eyes on your bags at all times. If you have to leave the bags, always designate someone responsible to keep watch. Airport security checkpoints are favorite target places. Be alert to your valuables while you pay for tickets at train stations.

- In public places and when using public transportation, women should hold their purses to the front, and men should put their wallets in their front pockets. Be especially alert to pickpockets in areas frequented by tourists. Fanny packs and backpacks are easily accessed by pickpockets. It is amazing how naive Americans are about pickpockets. Keep your valuables out of sight and your purse in sight.

I teach my groups to be alert to possible pickpockets. Often they are male, wear tennis shoes (so they can run fast if caught), and tend to shadow and follow the group. Or they try to stand in the middle of your group on public transportation. They sometimes work in teams where one distracts while the other robs you. Children and babies are often used. Anytime an out-of-the-ordinary distraction happens, your pickpocket antenna should immediately go up—such as two men loudly arguing, a fight, a baby making a scene, etc.

MONEY

Americans are sometimes surprised to learn that the dollar is not the medium of exchange all over the world. Each country has a different medium of exchange. This does not mean that dollars are not valuable—they are! But they must be exchanged into the national currency. Hotels, airports, train stations, and banks all have official exchange places.

Always exchange money in official exchange places which give a receipt or with your national host. In some countries you will need your passport in order to exchange. Never exchange on the street. On one trip, a team member ignored this and gave two men on the street a $100 bill for local money. Then they said that they could not divide a $100 bill. Could he give them two $50 bills? They gave him back the $100 wadded up and he gave them two $50 dollar bills. It was not long, however, till he discovered that they did not really give him back his $100 dollar bill. They gave him a $1 bill. By then it was too late and they were gone.

Credit cards and travelers checks are accepted in most Western countries. But these probably will not be accepted in most Third-World and second-world countries. Find out from your host in what form you need to bring money. Also, if you bring cash, be sure that the bills are good quality without tears, marks, and not badly worn.

If you carry a large sum of money, remember these three rules: Always carry it in a money belt; never show the money; and never talk about it. Don't forget that it is illegal to carry more than $10,000 cash out of the USA without declaring it and filling out some paperwork.

HOTEL SAFETY

When you arrive, always locate the emergency fire exits. Know where your key is if you have to make a fast exit, or an exit in the dark. Either leave it on your bedside table, or in the door lock. Always lock your door.

If you are alone, be very alert to who is around you when you are opening the door of your room. If you have a ground floor room with windows, or a room with an external balcony accessible to other rooms, then be sure that those windows and doors are securely locked. If you can't secure them, ask for a different room. If you enter your room and it looks like someone has been in there, or if the door or lock has been damaged, do not go in! Get away immediately! Special valuables should always be kept in the hotel safe.

Have a great trip. Stay healthy and stay safe!

CHAPTER 13

WHILE YOU ARE THERE

Here you are on the missions field with your team. "Toto, I have a feeling we're not in Kansas anymore." What now? In a perfect world, if you planned your work in advance, all you now have to do it to work your plan. However, it will not work out that smoothly. Now is when your leadership is most needed.

Your group will arrive tired and somewhat disoriented. They are bombarded with all sorts of new cultural stimuli and all sorts of changes from the plan. Leader, this is the moment you were born for! This is why they pay you the big bucks! Leader, lead!!!

The problem is that you are exhausted too. Remember, now that you are on the field, your primary job is to solve problems, make decisions, and take care of your team. Manage yourself properly and protect your time so that you can do this.

PROBLEMS, PROBLEMS, PROBLEMS

Your first job as the leader when you arrive on the field is as a problem troubleshooter. Are things OK? Do we need to make some changes? Ask questions. How is the housing? What about the ministry plan? Food issues? Safety/security issues? Transportation issues? Your job is to quickly uncover problems and solve them. The trip is too short to procrastinate. Don't ignore them.

I always think through the whole plan in advance and try to anticipate possible problems and solutions. What happens if the bags don't arrive at the airport? What do we do if our vehicle is not there to pick us up? What do we do if we have a poor quality translator? If you think these things through in advance, then you already have a plan in mind. Otherwise, you will find yourself wrestling with problems when your mind is fogged with jet lag and exhaustion. Always be thinking ahead. What is your plan B ?

SURPRISES

It should not be a surprise to you that you will encounter surprises when you arrive at your destination. Communication breakdowns, misunderstandings, cultural procrastination, administrative incompetence, and outright lying all work to create surprises when you arrive. Keep your voice low and hold your temper. Roll up your sleeves and find a solution. This is your job. In your training, you taught your team to be flexible. Now you need to be flexible. Find a way to turn the lemon into lemonade.

> "Accept the changes in your plans as coming from God, not coming from others. Be open to God's plan. Look for what God is trying to show you in the situation and how God is wanting to work through you."—Martha VanCise

BEHAVIORAL ISSUES

The stress of travel, lack of sleep, hard work, and close quarters with others often brings out either the best or worst in people. As leader you are going to deal with personality/relational conflicts, tardiness, complainers, murmurers, romantic entanglements, slackers, substance abuse, immoral or improper behavior, moodiness, outbursts of anger, and challenges to your leadership.

When you see behavioral problems, don't procrastinate. Deal with problems promptly. Nobody enjoys confrontation. And deal with them privately if possible. Most of these things should be covered in your team covenant that each person signed. You may only need to remind them of the commitment they made when they signed that covenant.

Team Spiritual Life

There is a tendency to neglect the inner life while on a project. As leader, help your team to stay closely connected to God. Remind them to begin each day on the field with a few quiet minutes of communication with God, Bible reading, and devotional reading. You might want to work with your team on a plan for this during the team training process. During the project, hold each other accountable by designating prayer/accountability partners.

If possible, hold daily team meetings while you are on the field. These should be short, but should include a short devotional, sharing, and prayer. They also are opportunities for announcements, troubleshooting problems, team business, and reminders.

Paying the Bills

It is best to have only one person responsible for paying bills and keeping financial records. This may be you as team leader or a designated team treasurer. Be very wise in keeping your team funds safe. Can you pay in US dollars or do you need to pay in the national currency? Don't wait until the last minute to find out. All expenditures should be receipted. Carry a box of envelopes to put payments in. Carefully keep all receipts and also keep careful accounting records.

How much money should you bring to the field to pay the team bills? This depends on whether or not you can write a check drawn on a US bank, use credit cards, or must use cold cash. Find these things out in advance.

Before departing the US, work out a very exact budget of expected expenditures. Then, add 20 percent! It is very, very bad form to get to the field and not have enough money to pay the team bills.

PHONE AND EMAIL COMMUNICATIONS

Many of your team members will want to communicate with family back home. Work with your host to come up with a plan to do this. Is there a way that you can have a team computer where team members can write emails? Is there a nearby Internet café? Do American phone cards work here? Do you know the access numbers? Can you buy local phone cards? How do they work? Where is a safe phone to use? Does your US cell phone work here and how much is the cost? If you call from the hotel, what is the cost? Each new mission location is a communication/technical challenge to understand and overcome. Oh yes, when calling home, don't forget the time difference!

As leader, it is wonderful if you can communicate with your team members by phone. It is difficult to manage a large team and troubleshoot schedules, logistics, and problems if you cannot communicate with your people and with your hosts. It is rare that your US phone will work overseas—and if it does, the cost probably is prohibitive. Also, realize that most US phones will not work overseas even if you change the chips.

The most common solution is to buy, borrow, or rent a cell phone (or phones) in the host country. You can buy a phone chip with a local phone number for very little. Then you buy a phone card that gives you a certain number of minutes. Your in-country host can help you with these things.

Should you take your laptop computer on the trip? It is a great way to keep the folks back home posted on developments, maintain prayer support, and keep family members from worrying. Some teams send daily updates back to their home church or to a group mailing list.

Your computer will probably work on both 110 and 220 power, but you will need a power plug adapter—to help you plug into their unique wall sockets. You might also need a special adapter to plug your standard telephone cord from your modem into their unique telephone sockets. Let your national hosts help you with these problems.

RELATIONSHIPS

Far more important than the actual work that they do are the friendships that team members build—both with fellow team members and with nationals. Who does God want you to especially befriend, disciple, and encourage on this project?

Some warnings and advice: Avoid cliques. Sit with different people at mealtimes and while traveling.

Be aggressive meeting people. The key to developing new friendships is asking questions.

Don't neglect talking to the children. Some tend to ignore children and focus only on the adults.

Use common sense in male/female relationships. Avoid romantic relationships. The mission project is too short and there is too much invested to have your focus and time distracted by romantic involvement. Save it for when you come home.

Romantic relationships with nationals are very tempting. Sometimes they work, but they are fraught with dangers and difficulties. Plus, the trip is too short to allow your focus to be distracted by romantic relationships. Remember, for most of the world, America is the Promised Land—the land of economic prosperity. Marriage to an American means US citizenship and economic prosperity. Don't ignore the giant language and cultural differences.

Gifts and Promises

Expect your team to have many problems concerning gifts and promises to nationals. Gifts unwisely given can create jealousy, expectations of additional gifts, greed, manipulation, begging, and dishonesty. It can create problems for the next team who does not give gifts. Talk to the missionary host and the team leader before giving money to anyone. Realize that you may be dealing with a culture where $100 is more than a month's salary. Imagine someone giving you a month's salary. Small gifts, carefully given, are the best policy.

Begging is a serious problem in Third-World countries. Every team member will have to wrestle with the ramifications of saying no. Will they reject me? Will I not be welcome to return? Are they only interested in my friendship for financial benefit?

Help your team to understand that there are some cultural matters involved. Your income is probably 60 times more than the employed African (and many are unemployed). In their culture, it is expected that those who have will help those who have not. That is the way Africa has functioned for generations. Culturally, it is entirely appropriate and expected for them to ask you for help.

On the other hand, when people ask you for something, it is OK to say no. However, it is important how you say no. It is better to offer excuses or postpone it for another time than to harshly say no. The classic cultural treatment of this subject is

African Friends and Money Matters written by David Maranz.

Promises. It is common to be asked to provide funds to finish a house construction, help pay for a child's schooling or school fees, help buy medicine for a sick child, sponsor a child to come to America to study, or give funds to bury a relative (some relatives are buried every time an American comes to town).

Also, be careful about promising to help nationals get into the US to study. Ninety percent will remain in America, no matter what they promised you. Furthermore, it is poor stewardship of mission dollars. Compare $10,000 spent for schooling a single national in the US (who probably will remain here) with $10,000 spent for church planting in a needy country. Also, are you contributing to the brain drain of the brightest, most gifted students in that country? They are needed much more in their country than selling used cars in America. Be careful of raising the hopes of the students. Encourage them to first pursue educational opportunities in their own country before studying abroad.

> "In most cases, it is unwise for us to directly help or even invite persons directly to come to the U.S. for study, etc. We are just not qualified to know who is most deserving after only a week of fellowship."—Dub Jackson

You may see your gift as a single, one-time supplementary gift. The national may take it as a promise of support for years. If you do give a gifts, be very explicit as to the terms. When you make a promise to a national, it is like making a promise to a child. If you tell a child maybe, they only hear a promise, not a possibility. We often have the tendency to make promises to be polite, just to get people off our backs—to put them off. You might tell a national to come see you if he or she ever visits America. Several months later the person may be on your doorstop with his or her bags prepared to live with you for an indefinite time.

> It is better not to make promises than to make promises and not keep them.

It is better not to make promises than to make promises and not keep them. Broken promises create bitterness, mistrust, and cynicism. One missionary complained about the team whose "mouths outran their wallets." Do not promise something you will not be able to carry out. Gather information, go home, and then decide what to do. This applies not just to personal gifts, but to possible funding by your home church of certain projects. Often we make promises on behalf of our home churches that we have no authority to make.

It is best to focus your gifts through the local church instead of through individuals. Give through organizations and not directly. Give church to church. Work through the missionary or your national host.

Some personal gifts are expected—hospitality gifts, tips to drivers, gifts to translators, gifts to host families, gifts to those who prepared meals. Give gifts that emphasize personal bonds of friendship. Give gifts not as payment for services, but just as expressions of friendship.

> "Team members see the enormous needs and make all kinds of promises while they are on the field. As soon as they get home, many people forget their promises. The locals do not forget."—Martha VanCise

Oh yes, one other thing: Be careful about giving out your home address or email address. You may receive a barrage of annoying requests for money and help.

CHURCH SERVICES

Americans are often utterly unprepared when they visit churches in other countries. They know that these churches are culturally different, but they aren't sure how they should act in this different environment. What are some things that we can do to make this experience better?

When You First Arrive. First impressions are very important. You often do not get a second chance to make a first impression. Meet the church leaders before the church service if possible. Smile and be friendly and express appreciation for the opportunity to visit. Find out the names of the leaders, especially the pastor and translator, and greet them by name. Work on remembering the names. Carry 3-by-5 cards and write the names down. It is often helpful to give the pastor your business card, as this will help him to remember your name, especially when he introduces you.

Talk beforehand with the pastor about the needs of the people and the problems. Also, ask him exactly what he wants you and your teammates to do and how long he wants you to take. Be very diligent to honor what he says about time.

Also, talk with the pastor about how to end the service. Some places do not give an invitation during the service. Other may give invitations, but do it differently. Inviting people to come forward, for instance, is not common in Romanian churches. It is better to ask people to raise their hands and then to meet you or the pastor at a clearly designated place in the front after the service.

Learn a few words of greeting in the national language. This says to the national believers how much you value their language and culture.

Encourage your team to meet the people before and after the service. You don't have to know the language to smile and greet someone. Avoid bunching up in a "holy huddle" and creating an "us" and "them" dichotomy.

Dress and Behavior in the Church. It is important not to offend your host church in your behavior or dress. You do not want anything to hinder their receptivity to the message that you have come to proclaim. Also, you don't want to hurt the testimony of your host or missionary who has brought you to the church.

There are wide cultural differences in dress and behavior in churches around the world. What you wear at church in America may not be appropriate in a little village church in Eastern Europe or in the African village. For instance, I love bright ties, but it would hinder my testimony in some Eastern

European churches. You don't have to make a fashion statement with your clothes. Remember, these people are often very poor. When you dress in your finest, you put distance between you and them.

The role, place, and dress of women is an especially sensitive issue. In some places in Africa it is more appropriate for a woman to show her breasts than to show her legs. In Eastern Europe, married women wear head coverings, no jewelry, and no makeup to church. Women should dress very modestly. In many places, women should wear dresses (not pants), little makeup, and no jewelry. Avoid sleeveless blouses, low-cut blouses, and tight-fitting clothes. Violation of these principles could hurt the testimony and witness of your entire group. One Sunday morning in Eastern Europe our team gathered in the hotel lobby to go to an Eastern European village church. One of the girls had on a low-cut blouse and I had to ask her to go back to her room and change. It embarrassed both of us.

Men and women often sit separately on different sides of the church. In Eastern European churches, it is considered wrong to write in your Bible or cross your legs if you are on the platform. Chewing gum or hands in pockets is wrong in some churches (and I've had youth do both at the same time!).

The best thing to do is to ask your host beforehand to steer you correctly. Also, during the church service, watch the people around you and imitate their behavior. Try to put yourself in the place of the average person in the pew. How do they see you? What are you saying through your dress, behavior, body language, and actual words?

Photo cameras and video cameras are usually OK in the church, but you need to be sensitive as to when you snap that picture and when you move around the church trying to get that special shot. Lord's Supper and invitation times are not appropriate.

Speaking in the Church. Most speaking opportunities involve a greeting, a testimony, or a sermon. Smile, look at the people, relax, and enjoy the experience. It is always good to begin your words with a greeting in their own language. What do you say to these people? Remember that people all over the world are the same. They have essentially the same needs, problems, desires, and dreams. Try to put yourself in their place and speak to their needs and interests.

Preachers need to preach the Bible, preach it clearly and simply, and end on time. Remember that preaching through a translator almost doubles the time of your message. Sometimes more is not better. It is just more. Good preaching in America will be good preaching anywhere in the world. Honor your hosts and the church you are visiting with good preaching. Come prepared. Give the people your best preachers. Avoid preaching on sensitive issues.

When you give a greeting or a testimony, keep it short. Introduce yourself and share something brief from the Bible or your personal experience that will encourage the people. One of my pet peeves is Americans who come to Eastern Europe and all they do is flatter or praise the people for what they have suffered. This has no edification value.

Music. If your team sings or plays instruments, be sure that the music is culturally sensitive. For instance, what we would call progressive music and rock music are unacceptable in many places of the world. You can seriously hurt your group's testimony by a poor choice of music.

Think communication when you are planning your music. Are you going to sing in their language? It is incredibly effective if you do. Find someone in your hometown who knows this language and have them help you to translate your music and teach you the pronunciations.

If you are unable to sing in their language, then be very sensitive in your choice of songs. If the national believers don't recognize the song and are unable to think the words in their own language as you sing or play it, then there is no edification value in your music. Therefore, choose older and traditional songs. Newer songs are not going to be known by the people. Again, check with your host beforehand concerning your music.

Interpreters

In many places, you will need interpreters to function and successfully carry out your mission. Sometimes they seem to be more interrupters than interpreters! Good ones can bless your trip and bad ones can hurt your trip. Problems with interpreters include romances, begging from the team, laziness, bad attitudes, and theft. In addition to competency in English, look for a servant spirit in an interpreter. Do they have the attitude of wanting to truly serve the Lord and also serve the team?

Never disrespect your interpreters. Learn their names. "Hey you!" is not OK. When asking them to do things, always ask with a respectful, "please." Ask cultural questions whenever in doubt and give them permission to correct you when you are making cultural goofs. If you must correct an interpreter or have a problem with him, do it privately and with respect.

It is a good idea to have an orientation meeting with your interpreters at the very beginning of the project and lay out your expectations and rules. Help them to see themselves as part of the team, not just "hired mouths."

Name Tags

Our American names are often strange, hard to remember, and hard to pronounce for the nationals that we are visiting and working with. Consider creating quality name tags for your team members. Have your team members wear them always, for they represent to the people who you are wherever you go. Also, providing name tags for the translators can help them to feel part of the team and help your team members quickly learn their names.

PHOTOGRAPHY

Photography is very important on a mission trip. Not only do you want to record your special memories, but you want to capture the trip in order to stir up interest in the hearts of the people back home. Some groups appoint a team photographer. Don't forget to take a group photo during the trip.

You may get the best photo opportunities of your life on this mission trip. Don't mess it up! Here are Kirby's Twelve (not Ten) Commandments for dummy photographers:

1. Know your camera before you take it on a trip.
2. You can't take that perfect shot if you don't have your camera with you.
3. Your camera and film always go in your carry-on bag, not in your checked bag. You don't want to know the consequences of violating this rule!
4. Always carry too much film and an extra battery.
5. Don't take photos at airports, border crossings, military installations, prisons, or police stations.
6. Ask permission when photographing strangers.
7. Always have a camera with zoom capability and use the zoom often. When taking photos of people, the closer the better. Fill the frame!
8. Avoid taking pictures into the sun.
9. Early morning and late afternoon are best for outdoor shooting.
10. Color rules! Look for colorful backgrounds and colorful photo subjects. Avoid boring backgrounds.

11. Take lots of pictures. You have to take a lot to get a few good ones!
12. People love pictures of people. And don't forget to include yourself in the pictures.

SHOPPING

It is important for teams (especially the women) to have some shopping time on the mission trip. It is not unspiritual. You are contributing to their economy, honoring their culture, and having fun. Do your Christmas shopping! You will get awesome deals on interesting things that have special meaning to you. If you see something you really like, then buy it. You may not see it anywhere else, or may not get another chance to shop.

Bargaining. You probably cannot bargain in shops, but it is expected with street vendors. Haggling is part of the fun of shopping in these countries. My bargaining policy in many places is to cut the asking price in half, and negotiate from there. The more you buy, the better deal you can negotiate. If you don't speak the language, have some paper and pen to write out prices. You may perhaps barter things such as pens, hats, flashlights, and watches. It is very helpful to have your translators and national helpers accompany you when you go shopping. Remember that you will have to pay US duty on any thing over $1,000 of purchases.

SIGHTSEEING

In 14 years of leading mission teams, I have met a few superspiritual saints who thought it was unspiritual to do any sightseeing on a mission trip. But for most team members, a little sightseeing is a special treat that they really enjoy. It does not make sense to come to Europe and not see any of the sights. It is a shame to go to Africa and not see the animals.

Attach a day of sightseeing at the end of the project. It provides a time for the team to unwind, play, process, and talk about the experiences of the week.

Sometimes, if the schedule permits, offer a sightseeing extension on a mission trip. The mission trip costs one price and the voluntary extension costs an additional price. People may choose only the mission trip; or if they have extra time and money, they may choose the extension also. This may be a side trip to Vienna, a stopover in Paris, or a safari in the Masai Mara.

JOURNAL YOUR JOURNEY

One of the most important things you can do during the short-term experience is to keep a journal. We remember what we record! Buy a small, spiral-bound notebook and keep it with you everywhere you go. Write down all that you do and everything of interest. Keep an accurate account of all names, places, and events. Don't just write down the facts. It is also important to record your feelings and emotions. You will not going to have time to spiritually digest all that occurs. A journal will help you in the digestion process. It will also give you a tool to use as you come home and try to relate your experiences.

> "Thoughts disentangle themselves when they pass through your fingertips."— Dawson Trotman

It is helpful to begin journaling before you leave on the trip. Don't forget to take advantage of the long airplane trip home to spend some extra time writing.

When you get back home, perhaps take time and type it up in a organized manner. Reviewing it in this manner will remind you of the lessons learned, of the things you wrote down that you needed to do upon returning, and of prayer needs.

Journaling Tips. In your journal, deal with things such as:

- What was the high point of today? Things that have happened today.

> "Those precious moments, the cherished memories, are what will keep the dream of mission work alive in our prayers and actions, as well as in the prayers of our partners in mission in the years ahead."—David Forward

- Interesting people that I met today.
- What work did I do?
- Unusual or funny things?
- Biggest frustration today.
- Problems I am dealing with.
- Prayer items or praise items.
- How am I feeling? What am I learning about myself? How am I changing?
- What do I need to do when I get back home? Promises made?
- What did God teach me today?
- Things I learned in my Bible reading time today. (See appendix 9.)

SAYING GOOD-BYE

> As you leave, are your hosts glad you came? Or glad you are going?

I hate good-byes, but my teams love them. You will never hear such weeping and wailing as when teams tell their national friends, host families, and translators good-bye. It is amazing *what* strong relationships have been forged in just a few days. Take some pictures. Exchange addresses. Hug and then hug some more. Don't be afraid to show your emotion.

CHAPTER 14

HOME AGAIN. WHAT NOW?

OK, you are now back home. Did you cheer on the airplane when you touched down on American soil? Did you kneel and kiss the ground when you got off the plane? My tradition is to get breakfast the next morning at Waffle House. Nothing is as "American" as Waffle House!

It's great to be home, but what now? Where do you go from here? What do we do with this experience? What does God want from us now?

The actual impact of the short-term mission experience should not be over after the short-term project is over. The great danger is that we see the short-term experience as an end rather than a means. If people don't do something in response to the volunteer experience in the first 60 days home, then they will lose what they have gained. We must do a better job helping people to refocus their lives in light of the changes that have occurred in them on a short-term trip. How do we help a team

> "The shocking thing to many team members is how quickly the experience happens. They spend three to four months preparing and two weeks experiencing."—Larry Ragan

member process and digest the impact of the trip that results in changed actions and a changed life? How do we help people apply this short-term experience for long-term life change? We need a purposeful plan and strategy. Please, please, don't neglect this vital element!

There is a great tendency for the team leader to think, "My job is over when I get the team home." I know because I used to do it. We tell people good-bye at the airport when we arrive home, and that's it! You must fight this. Your job is NOT OVER!

Let's begin with meetings. There are three things your team needs to do together once you get home: debrief, have a picture party, and report to the church.

DEBRIEF

Divers have to go through a time of decompression as they move from the environment deep under the ocean back to the surface. Your team also needs a time of decompression as they make the reentry back into their own culture. Debriefing is a time when team members can share with each other what God did on the short-term project and how they are now different. It is a time to help people work through their experiences, make sense of the trip, and solidify changes that need to be made and actions that need to be taken. It helps people to deal with the post-trip blues. It brings closure to the trip.

> If people don't do something in response to the volunteer experience in the first 60 days home, then they will lose what they have gained.

Jesus Christ debriefed His disciples after their first short-term mission trip (Luke 10:1ff.). He listened to their stories, reviewed the highlights, rejoiced with them, pointed out some relevant spiritual principles, and then led them in prayer praising God for what He had done (Luke 10:17–24).

Debriefing should be a private time for only the team members. Make it a required part of the short-term experi-

 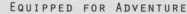

ence and try to do it very soon after arriving home. Plan on two to four hours of time. Invite the pastor to this meeting.

You want to facilitate sharing at this meeting. The less you speak as leader, the better. Help team members to verbalize and crystallize what they have learned and experienced and how they are different. Encourage them to honestly share their experiences, feelings, and impressions with each other. Pray together. A properly done debriefing session will brand the experience on their memories and will have an enormous long-term effect. Appendix 17 is a suggested meeting format and some helpful questions that will stimulate discussion.

Before this meeting, it is a good idea to give out trip evaluation forms. Give them out on the plane flight home. Have team members bring the completed evaluation forms to the debriefing meeting. You want to know three simple things:

- What did we do well?
- What can we do better next time?
- How is your life different because of this trip?

PICTURE PARTY

It is fun for the team to get together for a covered-dish meal and picture party not long after the project. Invite the spouses. Show a fun video of the project. If the time difference is not too great, call your overseas host during the party. Be sure to set this call up in advance with your friend overseas and arrange for the conversation to be on a speakerphone for all to hear.

Team members should get double copies of all their pictures and lay the extra copies on tables and let other team members take pictures they like.

REPORT TO THE CHURCH

Returning teams need to publicly report to the church on what God has done. Paul and Barnabas reported to their home church when they arrived back from a short-term mission trip. "When they had arrived and gathered the church together, they began to report all the things that God had done with them and how He had opened a door of faith to the Gentiles" (Acts 14:27 NASB).

Before you even depart on the mission trip, talk to your pastor and calendar a church service time when your team can share its report. He may give you an entire service or just a portion. Honor the time constraints he gives!

Quality reports can be of enormous benefit to the church in helping to personalize missions to the people. Look for every opportunity to share your story with individuals and groups. Poorly organized, rambling, lengthy, travelogue presentations will do more harm for the cause of missions in your church than good. Don't bore people with missions! You don't get a second chance to make a first impression. Do it well, or don't do it at all.

At all costs, avoid the talking head, long-winded, short-term speaker nightmare. People want the Cliffs Notes version, not the Amplified Bible version. Keep your report short and exciting. Tell them what God did and how the experience has affected you. One good story will accomplish much more good than a lot of exhortation. Remember, "Facts tell, but stories sell!" Be creative and involve different people in the presentation. You must use visuals, more than a long, boring slideshow. Communicate the mission through sounds, sights, touch, and even perhaps taste. Brainstorm as a team in advance on creative ways to share your story.

> Poorly organized, rambling, lengthy, travelogue presentations will do more harm for the cause of missions in your church than good.

Focus on the positive. Don't talk about all the problems, the cold showers, bugs, outhouses, the body odor, heat, uncomfortable beds, weird food, poor quality vehicles, etc. You want to encourage others to go next time, not discourage them!

EQUIPPED FOR ADVENTURE

THANK-YOU LETTERS

Not only should teams report to their churches, individuals need to report to their personal support teams. Hold your team members accountable to send thank-you letters to their partnership/support team helpers. If people prayed and gave, they deserve both thanks and a report. If I invested funds in a stock fund, and yet never heard any reports on my investment, I would probably be very angry. These people have invested in your team. They deserve to receive a report of what God did. Don't ever expect them to help again if they don't hear from you.

REENTRY EMOTIONS AND ATTITUDES

Reentry refers to returning home and reentering your own home culture. Many people have a hard time readjusting to life in America after a mission trip. Something changed very dramatically while you were overseas. You! It is hard to go back to living a normal life, as if nothing has happened. There is a sort of reverse culture shock. Martha VanCise shared this story: "One woman was so happy to get back to her clean modern kitchen that she kissed the kitchen floor; a few minutes later she was crying. Her cabinets overflowed with junk food, while children she had just left were dying from the lack of food."

The best way to deal with this is simply to be forewarned that this is a natural experience of many short-termers. Many others have also had to wrestle with the things you are feeling. You will work through it. Let's talk about some of the common emotions and attitudes.

- Physical and emotional exhaustion. "I have no energy. I don't want to do anything. I am emotional about everything. I am not sleeping well." What did you expect? You have been living on adrenaline the past few days, jetting around world, having the time of your life, and now you are home—exhausted, drained, and suffering from jet lag. Be patient. You'll get over it.

- Let down feeling. "I planned and looked forward to this trip for months. Now that it is over, I feel let down." Did the trip not meet your expectations or are you just disappointed that it is over? A lot of these feelings just come from the jet lag and physical/emotional exhaustion of the trip. Hopefully, you'll get over it in a few days.

- Anger at materialism. Anger at American affluence. "Everybody's lifestyle and values are wrong." You can't change America, but you can change you. We'll look at how later in this chapter.

- Frustration at misplaced church priorities. "How can my church spend $3 million to build a gym and yet can't give $5,000 to help build a church overseas? Why is 90 percent of my church's money spent on itself?" Hey, these are good questions. Maybe you can nudge your church to make some changes. We'll talk about how to do this later in this chapter.

- Boredom. You have been living on the edge for the past few day—jetting around the world. Now you are back to the humdrum and routine of your job and daily living. No wonder you are bored! Give it time. You'll adjust.

- Guilt over your own personal affluence and materialism. "I am so rich and they are so poor. It is wrong for me to have so much. Maybe I will sell everything I have, give it to the poor, and be a missionary." Whoa . . . let's slow down and talk about this. This trip should bring about changes in your life and priorities. But you (and your mate) need to work out a reasoned plan—not an emotional reaction.

- Arrogance. "I am now an expert on missions. I know how it is supposed to be done." One trip and you know more than missionaries who have given their whole lives. Dear prima donna brother, show a little humility! You are not as smart as you think you are. You have easy answers to hard problems. You don't have the expertise or experience to judge things. Missions professor Stan May writes, "Volunteers [must] remember that the career missionary knows the field better than they ever will."

- Disappointed with others who are not very interested in your experiences. "No one understands me. Why can't they see what I see now?" Instead of people dying to hear your story, they would rather die than to hear your story.

- Me, a Missionary? Fantasy. "Maybe I should be a missionary." Maybe this is not a fantasy! However, there is a giant difference between serving as a short-term missionary and living on the field permanently. The honeymoon is over quickly. A new missionary once wrote, "The short-term trip is over and the I-live-here part is sinking in. We are missing our families and would appreciate prayer." Serving as a vocational missionary is the greatest life in the world—if that is your true calling from God. How do you know? We'll talk about this later too.

Where Do I Go From Here— Personally?

This is the question that should be on the mind of your team members when they come home. "What do I do now? Where do I go with this?" Unless you do something about your experience, you will lose the experience in a couple of months. The goal is that the impact of the experience will last a lifetime. How do we help facilitate this? Here are a few ideas:

1. Begin by asking, "Why did God allow me to have this experience?" Short-term missions can be the first step to significant involvement in global missions. Unfortunately, for some it becomes the last step. They don't do anything else, or they settle for defining missions involvement only in terms of short-term trips.

   God gave you this experience for a purpose! Just as God gave men talents in the parable of the talents and told them to invest it (Matthew 25:14–28), God has given you this experience and expects you to invest it. This experience was far more than just a glorified Christian vacation or even just another ministry activity. God's intention is that the impact of this short-term trip last for a lifetime! It is an experience that God has allowed you to have for a purpose. You must discover that purpose. How?

   Begin by asking yourself, "What has God shown me during this experience? How am I different?" Ask people who have gone on mission trips, "How are you different now as a result of your short-term experience?" Their answer reveals a lot. A short-term mission experience is not like a good book you read and then put on the shelf and forget about. God had a purpose in your going. The mission trip was not the end, but just the means of God working out His purpose. Discover that purpose and then obey God. A good place to begin is by prayerfully rereading your trip journal.

2. Keep your promises. Did you make any personal promises on your trip? To keep in touch? To pray? To give? To send something? It is time to keep your word.

3. Evaluate your own personal spiritual commitment. What has God shown you about your personal relationship with Him? Is He truly Lord? Has He shown you some things in your life that are not right? Are there some changes that need to be made? What are those changes and what is your plan to implement them?

4. Continue in the disciplines that help you to grow as a Christian. Often, the prayer on our heart as we return home is, "Lord, use me." A better prayer is, "Lord, make me usable." Our usability will be in direct relationship to our maturity, holiness, and likeness to Christ. This is why we need to continue to pursue spiritual growth through the disciplines of worship, prayer, personal Bible study, devotional reading, service, evangelism, and Scripture memorization.

5. Determine to begin practicing a world Christian lifestyle. It is hard not to be affected by the superficiality and the waste we see here at home. This does not mean that you need to go on a crusade attacking others. It does mean that you may need to obey God and change some things about your life. How will this short-term experience affect the way you spend your money? Have you ever thought about living more simply so that others might live eternally? Have you thought about increasing your standard of giving instead of your standard of living?

   How will this experience affect whom you marry? How you spend your time? Your life goals and priorities? Make a commitment to change the way you live based upon what God has shown you on this short-term project.

6. Bloom where you are planted. It is wonderful that you were serving Christ overseas. How about now serving Him right where you are! How has God used this experience to open

your eyes to the local need around you? What are you going to do about it? You were willing to go 5,000 miles to tell people about Christ. How about now going next door to your neighbor?

7. Prioritize globally focused praying. You can continue to actually do global missions through intercessory prayer. We are just as surely to go into all the world in prayer as we are to go into all the world preaching. Your prayer is just as important as the missionaries' preaching. As a matter of fact, their witness probably will be in vain without your prayer behind it. Prayer gives wings to preaching. Without the plow of the believing prayers of the church, the gospel seed sown by missionaries will fall on dry, hardened ground. God has invited us to "ask of me, and I will make the nations your inheritance, the ends of the earth your possession" (Psalm 2:8). Buy a copy of *Operation World* to help you in your praying.

8. Read and educate yourself about global missions. You must add fuel to the fire to keep it burning and good missions books accomplish this. Check out the books listed in the resources guide in the back. My book, *World of Opportunity*, explains what missions is all about, what God is doing around the world, and how the average person can be personally and strategically involved.

9. Commit to serve as a missions mobilizer. What is a missions mobilizer? A missions mobilizer is one who purposefully seeks to influence people and churches to be more active and personally involved in global evangelization. A missions mobilizer is one who acts as a catalyst to help interest people in global missions. This can be done through personal lobbying, exercising missions leadership in your local church, organizing short-term teams from within your church, distributing missions literature, arranging ways to expose people to missionaries, and recruiting potential vocational missionaries.

What are the possibilities of your sharing about your trip at church? In Sunday School classes? Other churches? Civic clubs? Youth groups? VBS? Schools?

10. Should you go as a full-time vocational missionary? You need to wrestle honestly with the question of whether or not God wants you to go the next step and offer yourself to serve as a long-term vocational missionary. Are you willing to pray, "Here am I. Send me!" (Isaiah 6:8)? Are you willing to ask, "God, where in the world do you want me to be?"

Sometimes one person or couple from every team I lead soon senses a call to vocational mission service. Are you willing to entertain this possibility? Dawson Trotman, the founder of the Navigators, once said, "Never do a job which others can do or will do if there are important jobs that others can."

WHAT NEXT FOR OUR CHURCH?

The short-term mission experience needs to be evaluated—not only personally, but also corporately as a local church. "Why did God allow our church to have this experience? What does God want us to do next?"

Remember, the most effective short-term ministry is built around long-term partnering relationships. God may want you to follow up on the relationships that you started overseas and on the long-term project vision that God has given you. What is your follow-up plan? Returning short-termers must help the home church catch and build the long-term vision of the project. Keep the church updated so that they can continue to pray informed prayers for the people you worked with overseas.

"Finally, they made it . . . back . . . launched by God's grace and now safely home by God's grace. A good piece of work" (Acts 14:26, 27 *The Message*).

Were any promises made on behalf of your church? Financial commitments? Promises to pray? Promise to return? Keep your

Your Journey of Discipleship and Mission, published by Global Focus ([770] 529-8610) is a great tool for helping returning short-termers work through the next step. It is a four-week study that helps people understand their personal interests and giftedness and plug in to where they fit in kingdom work.

word. It is now time to put legs on your good intentions.

Do you intend to take a team back? Now is the time to put that trip on next year's calendar.

APPENDIXES

Appendix 1
Selected Short-Term
Missions Agencies/ Resources

1. Most major denominations have short-term programs and offices. Just go to the denomination Web page and go from there.
   Southern Baptist: going.imb.org/volunteer.asp
   United Methodist: www.umvim.org/home.htm
   Presbyterian Church of America: www.mtw.org/home/site/templates/

2. Most major interdenominational missions organizations have short-term programs and offices.
   www.finishers.org/resource/shorterm.php
   www.wycliffe.org/short-term/home.htm
   www.om.org/opportunities/ywam.org/contents/get_outreach.htm
   www.teamworld.org/Development/Opportunity/ShortTerm/teamserve.asp
   http://sim.org/ministry.php?fun=10&mid=sta

3. Some organizations focus exclusively on short-term mission projects.
   www.globalpartnershipministries.com
   www.stemintl.org

4. Some Web pages promote a variety of mission projects.
   www.mislinks.org/practical/shterm.htm
   www.shorttermmissions.com
   www.mnnonline.org/stmdb/
   www.intercristo.com
   www.adventures.org
   globalsharesystem.org/proto/index-f.htm

 EQUIPPED FOR ADVENTURE

Appendix 2
Is It Safe to Go on a Mission Trip?

People want to know, "Is it safe to go on a mission trip?" First, if people want to be safe, they should stay home. Travel always involves risk. Also, my Bible tells me that bringing the gospel to those who have not heard is never a safe thing to do. Missions is never safe, We have enemies.

On the other hand, we cannot allow fear to keep us from doing the work of God. If we are reduced to living in fear, then the terrorists win. Where is our faith? Danger does not change the Great Commission. If God is in control of our lives, and we are doing God's work, then whatever happens is in God's hands.

A pastor told me recently, "We are a little nervous about doing an international mission trip this year. Instead, we are going to do a project in Washington, D.C." I said, "Pastor, what do you think is the number one terrorist target in the world?" He replied, "Washington, D.C.?"

We need to be careful not to overreact in fear and caution. Ten million Americans went to Europe in 2004 and not one was killed by terrorists. Air travel security is tighter than it has ever been before. The next US terrorist target will not be an airplane or airport, but a softer, easier target such as a subway, tunnel, power plant, or high-rise building.

This is a strategic time in global history. The eyes of the world are on America. This is not a time to retreat into our shells and hide like turtles. People want to hear what Americans say. They want to know how our faith makes a difference in a time like this. Many of them are afraid and want to know if God has a word for us at this time. A nonreligious Jewish travel agent who helps my groups recently emailed me from Hungary, "What will happen in the near future? I am really afraid of a terrible war worldwide. What does the Lord say now?" Wow! Right now is an important time in history for us to go. The opportunities are greater than ever before!

In a way, the current events may separate those who really want to serve the Lord at a strategic time in global history, and those who only want to be "Christian tourists." It tests our motivations. These are the times that try men's souls! Have you read what the apostle Paul wrote? "But there is another urgency before me now. I feel compelled to go to Jerusalem. I'm completely in the dark about what will happen when I get there. I do know that it won't be any picnic, for the Holy Spirit has let me know repeatedly and clearly that there are hard times and imprisonment ahead. But that matters little. What matters most to me is to finish what God started: the job the Master Jesus gave me of letting everyone I meet know all about this incredibly extravagant generosity of God" (Acts 20:22–24 *The Message*).

Not only must we be brave, but we must also be wise. Therefore, having said all of this, I do promise to do all I can to keep my groups safe. This may mean flying foreign airlines, avoiding "tourist" places, avoiding Muslim areas, and teaching groups how to keep a low profile while traveling. There are almost nonexistent populations of Muslims in parts of Eastern Europe, and the Africa teams work in non-Muslim areas in the central highlands. People in all three of these countries love Americans.

The world has changed and this terrorist threat is not going to go away quickly. Those who think that they will wait this thing out until more favorable times will wait a long, long time. We will have to learn to live under this new threat situation for a long time. We are told that the probability is 100 percent of new terrorist incidents. We must not panic when these things happen. At a time when everything was coming unglued, Jesus told His disciples, "Do not let your hearts be troubled' (John 14:1)" God commanded Isaiah, "Say to those with fearful hearts, 'Be strong, do not fear.'" (Isaiah 35:4).

Safari for Souls
May 28–June 8, 2005, Kenya Team Application

Name (as on passport)_____

Passport number (if you have)_____Birth date _____

Address _____

City _____ZIP Code _____

Phone (home)_____(work)_____Email_____

Marital Status (single or married)_____Weight _____

Current or last employer (If student, name school.) _____

Position held _____

Church where you belong_____

Ministry presently held at your church_____

Ministry preference: ❑ women ❑ children ❑ youth ❑ music ❑ evangelism

❑ preach ❑ health care ❑ other _____

Spiritual gifts (if known) _____

Health concerns or disabilities? (If so, please detail on the back.) _____

Emergency contact name and phone _____

Insurance beneficiary _____

Two-day Safari extension? (y/n) _____

United frequent flyer # _____

Please attach (or email) (1) your personal testimony and (2) a brief recommendation from your Sunday School teacher or a church pastoral staff member, and (3) $100 nonrefundable application fee.

Dr. Scott Kirby, Global Partnership Ministries, 12195 Hwy 92, Suite 114-333, Woodstock, GA 30188; (770) 361-0705; MissionMatch@aol.com; www.globalpartnershipministries.com.

Appendix 4
Sample Team Member Covenant

I agree to cooperate with my team leaders concerning the work assignments, food, and accommodations provided for the team.

I agree to stay with the team from the beginning to end and carry my part of the load.

I agree to abstain from the use of alcohol, tobacco, improper language, and improper sexual conduct while on this mission.

I agree that in the event of an accident, illness, injury, or any other unforeseen emergency, I will not hold the team leader, hosting organization, other team members, project host, or my church personally responsible or bring any legal actions against them.

_____   _____
Name   Signature

_____   _____
Date   Witness

Appendix 5
Sample Prayer/Financial Partnership Record

Name	Address	City	State	ZIP Code	Email Address	Phone Number	Letter Sent?	Response?	Gift Amount	Thank-You Sent?

Appendix 6
Sample Prayer Support Letter

Dear Clyde:

God has opened up an opportunity to be part of our church's mission team to Kenya in May. I am so excited about this! We will be working in small villages telling people about Christ. I feel that God very clearly told me to go.

This is a big thing in my life, and I need a team of friends behind me praying and helping. Would you consider being part of my mission partnership team?

Here are some things I need you to pray about.

1. I will be spiritually prepared for this work.
2. God will provide the $2,395 I need for this trip.
3. We will all be safe and healthy on the trip.
4. The people we work with will be responsive.
5. God will watch over my family while I am gone.

If you think you can be part of my mission partnership team, then please mail the enclosed form back to me in the envelope provided.

Sincerely in Christ,

Scott Kirby

Appendix 7
Sample Prayer/Contribution Response Card

_____ Yes, I will pray for _____ and the mission.

_____ I want to help with the following gift (enter amount) _____.

Make check payable to Global Partnership Ministries and return to participant in the enclosed envelope. Do not write participant's name on check. All contributions are tax deductible.

Name _____

Phone number _____

Address _____

City/State/ZIP Code_____

Email address _____

_____ Yes, I will pray for _____ and the mission.

_____ I want to help with the following gift (enter amount) _____.

Make check payable to Global Partnership Ministries and return to participant in the enclosed envelope. Do not write participant's name on check. All contributions are tax deductible.

Name _____

Phone number _____

Address _____

City/State/ZIP Code_____

Email address _____

Appendix 8
Sample Team Meeting Schedule

Date/Time/Place	Topics to Cover	Assignments
Session #1 Date _____ Time _____ Place _____	**Overview and Prayer Letter** *Review project details, overview * Passports * Application form given out * Review team meeting schedule *Discuss prayer/support letters	Passport applied for? Prayer/support Letters application form completed
Session #2 Date _____ Time _____ Place _____	**Team Building/Introductions** *Passports? *Prayer/support letters sent? to team members: Country, *Introductions Game: Pair people up and History, customs/traditions, have them interview each other and write religion. out information about that person. Then introduce *Review team covenant and tha person using your notes. sign *Attitudes and expectations * Financial matters * Team policies/covenant * Prayer in small groups	*Assign report presentations

Session #3

Date _____

Time _____

Place _____

Culture Stuff

*Report presentations

* Discuss culture issues .

* Practice language phrases

* Prayer in small groups

Complete gift edness/interests Survey, bring next meeting

*Prepare personal testimony

Session #4

Date _____

Time _____

Place _____

Ministry Planning

* Collect giftedness surveys

* Plan ministry

* Personal testimonies

*Prayer in small groups

*Ministry teams meet

* Gather ministry supplies

Session #5

Date _____

Time _____

Place _____

Travel, Packing, and Health

*Frequent flyer stuff

*Packing tips/ baggage stuff

*How to stay healthy and safe

*Discuss packing list

*Get frequent flyer number

*Ministry teams meet

Session #6

Date _____

Time _____

Place _____

Last-Minute Stuff

*Review ministry plans

*Airport departure plans

*Final financial matters

Session #7

Date _____

Debriefing

Time _____

Place _____

Session #8

Date _____

Picture Party

Time _____

Place _____

Session #9

Date _____

Church Presentation

Time _____

Place _____

Appendix 9
30-Day Bible Reading Program

DAY	TOPIC	BIBLE READING
1	Spiritual Renewal for Service	Psalm 51
2	Taking Time to Pray	Mark 1:35–37
3	The Word and the Way	Psalm 119
4	The Power to Serve	Acts 1:1–12; Ephesians 5:18
5	Blessed to Be a Blessing	Psalm 67
6	Here I Am. Let Me Go!	Isaiah 6:1–12
7	Attitude of Humility	Philippians 2:1–16
8	Availability Plus Christ	John 6:1–14
9	Empowered to Serve	Matthew 28:16–20
10	The Lost Sheep/Coin/Son	Luke 15:1–32
11	The Unlikely Witness	John 4:1–42
12	The Harvest	Matthew 9:36–38
13	Spiritual Courage	Acts 4:1–31
14	Revive Us Again	Psalm 85
15	Overcoming Difficulties	Numbers 13:25–33
16	Jesus's Travel Advice	Luke 10:1–20
17	True Greatness	Matthew 20:20–28
18	Abiding in Christ	John 15:1–11
19	Facing Your Fears	Luke 12:22–34
20	Peace in the Storm	Philippians 4:8–20
21	Lessons from Jonah	Jonah 1:1–3; 3:1–10; 4:1–11
22	Serving with Gladness	Psalm 100
23	Loving the Lost	John 21:15–23
24	Dedicated Service	Romans 12
25	Getting Along with Others	1 Thessalonians 5:11–18
26	Calling and Obedience	Genesis 12:1–4
27	God's Wisdom	1 Corinthians 1:18 to 2:5
28	The Power of the Word	Romans 10:9–17
29	The Word Became Flesh	John 1:1–18
30	Proclaiming Liberty to the Captives	Isaiah 6:1–6; Luke 4:16–21

Appendix 10
Sample Prayer Guide

Missions Prayer Guide

1. Prayer. Use the ACTS model (adoration, confession, thanksgiving, supplication). Some prayer items for your STEM prayer list:
   *Personal empowerment and enablement
   *Godly and servant attitudes
   *Those you will minister to
   *Your other team members and national hosts
   *Health
   *Safety in travel
   *Personal flexibility
   *Opportunities to share the gospel

Appendix 11
Sample Mission Team Ministry Preparation

1. CHILDREN'S MINISTRY

You've heard of the 10/40 Window. But have you heard of the 4/14 Window? The world's most fruitful mission field is not a particular place. It is not a particular country. It is children aged 4–14.

Craft Resources
www.ssww.com
www.gospelcom.net
www.childrensministry.net
www.faithresoucecenter.com/frc

For example, if you are doing a Bible school, you might prepare four 1½ hour preparations for about 40 children each day. Prepare for elementary-aged children (6–12 years old). Be prepared for children under 6 and over 12 also. If the group is large, you need to be prepared to break into age-graded groups working concurrently.

Each preparation should include music/singing, Bible story with visuals, crafts, games, and refreshments. You must bring your own crafts (instant camera, paint caps). Remember, all of this will be done through translation.

HINTS:

a. Music. Write songs on large poster board for the children to read. Let the children teach you some of their songs.

Five Major Elements:
Bible story
Crafts
Music
Games
Refreshments

b. Involve the national helpers/teachers all you can.

c. Consider decorations such as streamers, balloons, etc.

d. Practice your VBS before you go.

e. Choose a theme: a topic, theme, Bible story, or Bible character. Then design all materials accordingly (puppets, decorations, crafts, lessons, music, costumes).

f. Visuals, visuals, visuals. Puppets. Flannelgraph.

g. Expect more to attend than you planned for. Have name tags for all.

2. YOUTH

Prepare for several things:

    a. Outdoor sports and game activities (soccer, basketball, Frisbee)

    b. A youth evangelistic meeting. Testimony, speaker, music. Perhaps a pizza/soft drink party.

3. WOMEN

    a. A women's evangelistic tea. Held on Saturday afternoon. Bring gift bag for each woman, specialty teas, special cookies, and chocolates. Program should be testimony, gospel presentation, and encouraging women to meet together regularly for sharing, prayer, and Bible study.

    b. Also prepare a small-group Bible/discussion program for women to possibly be held one evening.

4. PUBLIC SCHOOLS

It is very possible that you will be able to speak in some public schools. Be sensitive to the headmaster's requirements concerning what kind of witness you may have. Can you offer a gift to the school? (special book, computer) Be prepared to speak on some of the following topics. Avoid politics or Iraq.

    a. How September 11 Has Changed America

    b. Schools and Student Life in America

    c. How Americans Think: Culture, Recent History, and Politics

    d. Why the Bible Is Important to Me

    e. American Literature

    f. American History

    g. An English-Language Workshop

5. EVANGELISM

Each team member should be trained in how to lead a person to Christ. Also, the team should be prepared to help teach others how to lead people to Christ. Tools may include gospel tracts, gospel bracelets, Evangecubes (www.evangecube.org).

6. PREACHING

Each team should have several people prepared to preach in churches. You never know how many different opportunities will arise. In villages, messages should be very basic and simple. (See notes on how to speak through a translator.) Talk to your national host first and find out do's and don'ts, time limits, proper dress for a speaker, expectations, audience, and invitation traditions.

Sermon Preparation for Rookie Preachers
Before you begin, remember to keep the message simple (KTMS), tell basic stories, and consider the audience. (See David Forward, *The Essential Guide to the Short-Term Mission Trip*, 118–20.)

a. Choose your subject and/or Scripture passage. (i.e., the Resurrection, Zacchaeus, prodigal son).

b. Give me three examples of how it has affected your (or someone's else's) life.

c. Now answer the questions, "How? So what? Who cares?"

7. CHRISTIAN ARTS
How to Effectively Use Drama and the Arts in Volunteer Missions
Clowns, photography, dance, drama, skits, puppets, mime, painting. Shadow shows.
http://www.fetchbook.co.uk/fwd_topics/id_1540562.html
www.gospelcom.net
www.onewaystreet.com

8. PRAYERWALKING
www.waymakers.org, http://www.iphc.org/mm/praywalk.html
Books: *Prayerwalking* by Steve Hawthorne and Graham Kendrick (Lake Mary, FL: Creation House, 1993)
Prayer Journeys: A Leader's How-To Manual; order from Caleb Project.
Follow Me: Becoming a Lifestyle Prayerwalker by Randy Sprinkle (Birmingham, AL: New Hope Publishers, 2001)
There are numerous books on this. Check out www.amazon.com.

9. MUSIC

www.gospelcom.net/cef/

Signing as someone sings

10. MEDICAL

Nutrition classes, AIDS education, sex education, health-care clinics, eye care, dental clinics.

11. SPORTS MINISTRY

Ultimate Frisbee.

12. SKILL CLASSES

Teach Some Skill Plus a Bible Study

Agriculture, conversational English, computer, carpentry, electrical, accounting, business management, starting a small business, auto repair, sewing, signing for the deaf, entrepreneurship.

Resources:

STEM "Ministry Activity Preparation Packet"

Appendix 12
Sample Personal Testimony
Preparation Work Sheet

TESTIMONIES

Consider writing out your personal testimony and having it translated and printed before you go into the language of the people you will be working with.

Also, each person should be prepared to share short (perhaps four-minute) testimony on each of these four topics. (See Rick Warren, *Purpose Driven Life*, 289–95).

a. Salvation Testimony. "How I Became a Christian"

b. Life Lessons. "The Most Important Lessons God Has Taught Me"

c. Godly Passions. "The Issues God Has Shaped Me to Care About Most"

d. Gospel Presentation. "The Gospel and How to Be Saved."

GENERAL ADVICE.

- A testimony should be like sausage—you can cut it to whatever length is needed.
- In most situations, short is sweet!
- Leave out sex stories and divorce issues.
- In some cultures, don't emphasize coming to Christ and baptism as a child.
- "If in doubt, leave it out."
- Authenticity and honesty cover a multitude of communication sins.
- Careful about slang! "We were at a rock concert and we were all going crazy!"
- Don't talk about God calling you to go on this mission, how much it cost, and how God provided the money. Avoid talking about money.
- Practice your testimony by giving it to other team members and getting their input.

TESTIMONY WORK SHEET

I. Introduce Yourself. (name, where you live, your profession, why you came)

II. Your Life Before Becoming a Christian

III. How You Became a Christian

IV. How Being a Christian Has Changed and Impacted Your Life

V. How Others Can Also Know Christ

Appendix 13
Hints for Speaking Through a Translator

Unless you know the national language, much of your ministry will be through a translator or an interpreter. I call them interrupters! Most people have never done this, so there are a few things to remember as you approach this new experience.

1. Go over your Scripture text, your message outline, and any possibly confusing points with your translator before the service. I also like to talk through my illustrations with the translator beforehand in order to avoid confusion later. Stories can crash and burn quickly if the translator gets confused as you tell it.

2. Look at the people, not the translator. Remember, you are speaking to the people, not the translator. The translator is simply your Aaron mouthpiece to bring the message that God has put on your heart to the people.

3. Relax and speak from your heart. I can remember one American pastor who was very nervous speaking through a translator the first time. Frankly, he was utterly boring. Never fear, however. The translator saved the day by taking the American's words and enhancing them with his own sermon. You know you are in trouble if the translator is taking several minutes to translate one sentence!
   Passion and sincerity communicate in any language. Concentrate on communicating the message that God has put on your heart. Stories are very effective—especially personal stories.

4. Speak in full phrases and sentences. Don't stop between subject and verb. Also, enunciate your words clearly and speak slower than normal. Slower, not louder!

5. Remember the time. Speaking through a translator almost doubles the time it takes to say something.

6. Avoid words that the translator might not understand. This means don't use King James English such as "Be of good cheer!" Assume that the translator has about a third-grade American reading and speaking ability so be very simple in your words.

7. Avoid culturally irrelevant stories. One preacher gave a long illustration about playing golf and getting a hole in one. It was a great story but completely out of place in a country where there are no golf courses. The people didn't have a clue what he was talking about.

8. Be careful with jokes. They rarely translate well and can be easily misunderstood. Always review the joke or funny story with your translator before the service to be sure that it will work. Generally avoid humor. This is also true concerning politics.

9. Remember that alliterations usually will not translate alliterated. Alliterations that are not exact often can be mistranslated. Also, remember that poetry and hymns do not translate effectively. Avoid quoting these.

10. Avoid having the interpreter translate passages of Scripture that you quote or read. It is better to simply tell the translator to read the verse or passage from his own Bible to the people instead of having him translate your reading of the Scripture.

11. Avoid American slang.

Translator Skit

Speaker

1. Tell them I am pleased to be here.

2. When you asked me at lunch to speak to you today, I had butterflies in my stomach.

3. But now I'm really happy to have this opportunity to be with you.

4. I'd like to talk with you today about the contextualization of theology in the Third-World setting.

5. But first let me share with you my testimony.

6. When I was just a kid . . .

7. I didn't understand the implications of what Christ did for me when He died on the Cross.

8. But then He convicted me of sin through His Holy Ghost.

9. I had been a real lady-killer. I lived a life of sex, booze, and drugs.

10. He set me free.

11. He made me a new creature. (excited, faster, and louder)

12. Now I have a new life. I'm forgiven my past. I am part of the body of Christ. They are my family. I'm so excited. I want to tell you all about it.

Translator

1. He says to tell you that she's very happy to be here.

2. At lunch I ate some flies that was in the butter, and now it is in my stomach while I am trying to speak to you.

3. It's OK. I'm really happy to have a chance to eat them with you.

4. I'd like to talk to you about a text from another world.

5. First I want to share my . . . ???

6. When I was just a small goat . . .

7. I did not understand what happened when Christ died at the intersection.

8. But a ghost arrested me for it.

9. I had killed a lady. Oh, I'm too embarrassed to translate what he just said. But then he took medicine and got better.

10. I was let go.

11. I was made into a new animal.

12. He's very happy. Please clap for him.

Appendix 14
Words and Phrases You Should Learn

It honors those that you are working with when you learn a little bit of their language. It is amazing how much love and care you can communicate with just a tiny vocabulary.

How do you find and learn words and phrases of the language you will be working with? There are several possibilities.

> **Language Book Online Sellers**
> www.amazon. com
> www.barnesandnoble.com
> www.ebay.com
> www.overstock.com

1. Find someone who can tutor you and your group.
2. Go to your local bookstore or buy online.
3. Search your language online.
   www.ipl.org/div/kidspace/hello
   www.mylanguageexchange.com

What do you need to know how to say?

Hello.	Good night.
My name is _____	Good-bye.
What is your name?	Where?
Yes.	More.
No.	I don't understand _____.
Toilet?	Pardon me.
Thank you.	Water.
Good.	How much does it cost?
Good day.	Very good!
Good morning.	How are you doing?

If you are really motivated, learn how to count to 100 in your new language.

Appendix 15
Sample Packing List

❏ Bible

❏ Passport/visa and copy of passport

❏ Airplane tickets

❏ Basic clothing

❏ Sunday clothes (jacket and tie for men, dress for women)

❏ Washcloth

❏ Hat

❏ Camera, extra film, extra battery

❏ Roll of toilet paper

❏ Insect repellent

❏ Antibacterial hand cleaner/hand wipes

❏ Earplugs

❏ Penlight

❏ Watch (Leave valuable jewelry at home.)

❏ Feminine products

❏ Medicines/medical kit (Take all you need because you probably can't buy in-country.)

❏ Journal for quiet times/record keeping

❏ Walking shoes

❏ Teaching notes/supplies, spare pens

❏ Sunglasses

❏ Rain poncho

❏ Sunscreen/lip balm

❏ Tissues

❏ Plastic grocery bags (for packing)

❏ Gifts for host pastor/wife and translator

❏ Reading material for airplane

❏ Extra eyeglasses, especially if you wear contacts

❏ Light jacket

❏ House shoes/flip-flops

❏ Money belt

❏ Bag of hard candy to give to children

❏ Snack items

❏ Travel alarm

❏ Small backpack

❏ Refillable water bottle

 212

Appendix 16
Sample Travel Medical Kit

❑ Ibuprofen (headache, muscle ache, inflammation)

❑ Aspirin

❑ Sleep aid

❑ Benadryl (allergic reaction, bee sting, pollen/allergies, itching, sleep aid.
   Carry this in both cream and pills.)

❑ Zilactin (mouth sores, ulcers)

❑ Cold medications (vitamin C, zinc tablets, favorite cold symptom reliever)

❑ Allergy/sinus medicine

❑ Antinausea medicine

❑ Antidiarrheal

❑ Motion sickness medicine

❑ Antacid

❑ Muscle pain cream

❑ Sore throat lozenges

❑ Antibiotic cream/ointment

❑ Laxative

❑ Antibiotics

❑ Thermometer

❑ Moist antibacterial towelettes

❑ Bandages

❑ Flexible bandage for joint sprains

❑ Saline eyedrops to flush eyes and get out dust

Appendix 17
Sample Debriefing Meeting Format and Questions

Consider meeting in a home for dessert or potluck dinner.

In your debriefing meeting discussion, you want to cover two broad areas. Under each of these areas are some questions to provoke discussion and thought.

1. How has this trip changed you? What have you learned?
   - How is your life going to be different as a result of this experience?
   - What one story or experience sums up the mission trip for you?
   - What was the most exciting thing that you saw God do?
   - What things about your host country do you now miss?
   - Talk about one special person you met on this trip and why.
   - What surprised you about yourself on this trip?
   - What attitude has surprised you about yourself since you have been home?
   - What was one cultural difference that you experienced?
   - What was the biggest surprise of the trip?
   - What was the funniest moment?

2. Where do you go from here? What do we do with this experience?
   - What changes do you intend to make in your life as a result of this trip?
   - What does our church need to do now?
   - What promises have we made that we need to fulfill?

Final comments by group leader. As you consider where to go now, there are three words to think about.

Prayer. How will this trip change your prayer life. What do you need to do now?

Share. How will this trip change your missions giving?

Dare. For some people, a short-term trip crystallizes a long-term vocational missionary call. Talk about this issue with the group.

EQUIPPED FOR ADVENTURE

New Hope® Publishers is a division of WMU®, an international organization that challenges Christian believers to understand and be radically involved in God's mission. For more information about WMU, go to www.wmu.com. More information about New Hope books may be found at www.newhopepublishers.com. New Hope books may be purchased at your local bookstore.

other missional-focused books

Trolls & Truths
*14 Realities About
Today's Church That
We Don't Want to See*
JIMMY DORRELL
ISBN 1-59669-010-0

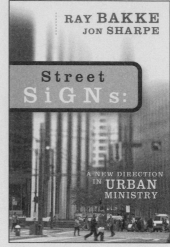

Street Signs
*A New Direction
in Urban Ministry*
RAY BAKKE and
JON SHARPE
ISBN 1-59669-004-6

A guide for Christians
who want to bring
spiritual and practical
transformation to
their cities.

**Families
on Mission**
*Ideas for Teaching Your
Preschooler to Love,
Share, and Care*
ANGIE QUANTRELL
ISBN 1-56309-991-8

Fun family activity
ideas that will help
teach preschoolers
how to love, share,
and care about others.

For information about these
books or any New Hope
products, visit us at
www.newhopepublishers.com.

new
hope
PUBLISHERS